The Pennine Way

A Walker's Guide

Acknowledgements

I am grateful to Sylvia Franks, former Chairman of the Pennine Way Council, for her help and assistance in compiling the information on Tom Stephenson and the history of the Pennine Way.

A huge thank you also to Mandy, my wife, who has provided companionship along my various Pennine Way trips, encouragement to complete this book and editorial support.

Dedication

To *Tom Stephenson*, without whom there would be no Pennine Way to enjoy.

The Pennine Way

A Walker's Guide

Chris Sainty

Photographs: © Chris Sainty (unless otherwise indicated)

Cover photograph: Summit of Deer Play, Northumberland

A catalogue record for this book is available from the British Library

Walkers' rights and responsibilities
The Pennine Way is a National Trail and walkers have a responsibility to familiarise themselves with their rights and responsibilities. Information about rights of way, Open Access Land, and the Countryside Code can be found at: *http://www.naturalengland.org.uk.*

Disclaimer
Every effort has been made to ensure that the information in this book is accurate and as up to date as possible. The author or publisher cannot however accept any responsibility for any inconvenience, accident, injury or loss sustained by anyone as a result of following the advice in this guide.

First published 2014 by DB Publishing, an imprint of JMD Media Ltd, Nottingham, United Kingdom.

ISBN 9781780913797

Printed and bound by Copytech (UK) Limited, Peterborough.

Contents

Introduction

The Pennine Way, Britain's first long distance footpath was opened on 24 April 1965. Nearly fifty years on, it continues to attract individuals and groups from around the world, to accept the challenge of walking from Edale in Derbyshire, to Kirk Yetholm in Scotland. The route described in this book is 254 miles long, but if you walked every foot of the National Trail which makes up the Pennine Way (the whole of the Bowes Loop, the Cheviot, and both the high and low level routes in Scotland) the total distance walked would be 268 miles.

"But that is really what the Pennine Way is all about – that the mass of the people should have the right to roam, rather than the few should restrict access so that they might indulge in their senseless slaughter.

That is why the Way starts at Kinder Scout, rather than as he (Wainwright) suggests, at Axe Edge. For Kinder was the cockpit of the battle for access. I must admit, though, that some of my friends and supporters would have taken the Way round Kinder rather than face the Enemy."

Tom Stephenson (*Pennine Way Council Newsletter*, No.19, Autumn 1985)

A number of books have been written about the Pennine Way, each offering something slightly different to the reader.

What this book aims to provide:
1. A uniquely detailed written description of the route from south to north, including points of interest along the way, which can be used in conjunction with Ordnance Survey (OS) or other maps.
2. Rarely seen documents on how the Pennine Way came into being.

3.   Spectacular photographs that provide a visual insight into the National Trail.
4.   A comprehensive list of books published on the Pennine Way.

This book is aimed at people who may be planning to walk the Pennine Way; those wishing to reminisce and reflect on their own particular journey along the backbone of England; or individuals who have an interest in the Pennine Way, but may never actually walk it.

If you can afford to spend three weeks walking the Pennine Way (even if this involves two or more separate visits) it is well worth it, as it is an experience that should not be rushed. The reality is that for many, the time and resources at their disposal may necessitate a faster traverse. It is however possible to set your own timeline and daily stopping points using this guide as a framework.

The route description is divided into 19 sections, which takes into account those points where accommodation and transport are more readily available. If you don't overextend yourself you will increase your likelihood of completing the Pennine Way as the daily mileage ranges from 6.7 miles along Hadrian's Wall, to 19.4 miles between Dufton to Alston via Cross Fell. Most days are 13–16 miles which allows time for a true appreciation of the splendour and variety of the landscapes you will be travelling through.

The detailed route description forms the majority of the content of each of the 19 sections. Place names on the route have been high-lighted in bold for ease of reference. Items of interest are separated from the route description within shaded boxes. At the beginning of each section is a photograph which captures an essence of that day's walk. The Pennine Way has a huge variety of signage along its 268 miles, and each of the photographs aims to show this diversity, because, surprisingly, they do actually add to the character of the Trail.

It can be difficult measuring mileage and height gained when using non-electronic tools. It is inevitable that some slight errors may creep in, especially when measuring distances between 83 selected points between Edale and Kirk Yetholm. Height gained between two points isn't an exact science. You only have to compare various guidebooks on the Pennine Way to see that every author has different figures. I have endeavoured to accurately include each contour line and the terrain between when measuring the total height gained or lost between two points. The height gain only relates to the Pennine Way. Walkers will need to add height gained and lost when leaving the route to find overnight accommodation. This can be a few feet / metres in some places but several hundred feet / metres elsewhere. For example, Windy Gyle on the Scottish Border ridge is at 2,030 feet / 619 metres, Cocklawfoot to the west is at 764 feet / 233 metres, and Barrowburn to the east is at 820 feet / 250 metres. If you come off the ridge for overnight accommodation you will need to regain any height lost the following morning when you walk back up to Windy Gyle.

It is impossible for any guidebook to be totally accurate as the Pennine Way is a 'living footpath'. The topography won't change but the team from Natural England who manage the footpath are constantly maintaining and improving the trail. Kissing gates are replacing ladder stiles in some areas as they are easier for walkers with Pennine Way packs to pass through. Similarly slabs may be removed or laid, new sections of duckboards may appear or disappear, and footbridges may be replaced. I have got into the habit of spending some time on the Pennine Way almost every year but things can change between my trips. If you spot any errors or changes, please let me know as I am keen for this book to be as accurate as possible.

What this book does not cover:
This guide does not set out to give the reader specific details on equipment; when it is best to walk the Way; or information on accom-

modation or transport in relation to walking the Pennine Way. This information is essential to your planning, but it can be readily found on the internet or elsewhere.

As maps are not included in this book, it is imperative that any walker takes appropriate and sufficient maps with them, and that they are competent in the use of a map and compass. The Pennine Way is a serious and potentially dangerous undertaking. It therefore cannot be overemphasised that anyone attempting the Pennine Way should have some experience in walking in open countryside, and have a good level of fitness as they will be walking continuously for 2–3 weeks carrying a pack. If you are unable for any reason to reach your intended overnight accommodation, please contact them but, bear in mind, that a mobile phone signal may only be available in areas of high elevation. Solo walking is only recommended for the most experienced walkers.

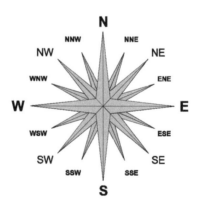

Cairn on Cross Fell – September 2009

A final thought...

The Pennine Way is a fantastic way of exploring England and the Cheviots, whatever your motivation. The landscape you walk through, the highs and lows (topographically, physically and psychologically), and the people you will meet on the way will make this an experience that you will be unlikely to forget. Who knows, like me, you may find yourself returning to the Pennine Way to see the parts that mist or rain obscured on your first visit, or to see the heather in its full autumn glory, or perhaps even just to do it all again!

Tom Stephenson

Tom Stephenson 22 June 1985 (aged 92 years) on Malham Lings celebrating 20 years of the Pennine Way and 50 years of his article, 'Wanted – A Long Green Trail'

Tom Stephenson was born in Chorley Lancashire on 12 February 1893, the eldest of nine children. He began his working life at the age of thirteen, working in a calico printing works two miles away from his home in Whalley, serving an apprenticeship as a hand printer in textiles, working a 66 hour week (illegally). He would often stand on the steps of the workshop looking up at Pendle Hill and the surrounding fells. One Saturday in February very early in his working life, (he was still thirteen at the time), he set off and climbed to the top of a snow-covered Pendle Hill, overlooking the Ribble Valley. From there he could see the skyline which included the Bowland Fells, Pen-y-ghent, Ingleborough, and Fountains Fell, and he became entranced by them and was determined to know them all better. That was the beginning of his love of walking, which continued throughout his life.

The next milestone in his life was when he joined Clitheroe Public Library. His first book was Charles Darwin's *Origin of the Species* which took him over a year to read, but it started off his interest in geology.

In 1915, when he was eighteen, he began night classes at Burnley Technical School, cycling the eight miles from Whalley each way on a second hand bicycle. After four years study (four evenings a week) he won a scholarship in geology at the Royal College of Science in London (now Imperial College). World War One was being fought in Europe, and Tom, an active member of the Labour Party had registered as a conscientious objector, as he held strong socialist and pacifist beliefs. Initially, at a tribunal in Clitheroe, he was granted an absolute exemption. However later, when more soldiers were needed for France, he was brought before a tribunal again where his case was reviewed. When he again refused to enlist he was arrested, fined forty shillings, and taken down to Plymouth by the 3rd East Lancashires and court-martialled. He was sentenced to twelve months in prison during which he used his time to read, amongst others, political books which served him in good stead in later life.

Tom spent his time in Wormwood Scrubs and following a second court-martial, he was additionally given two year's hard labour in Northallerton. When the war was over, and Tom was released, he had lost his scholarship so he went back to his old trade of block printing. He was an Independent Labour Party agent at Dartford in Kent for two years, and from 1922 onwards he spent eleven years at the Labour Party's headquarters running the Directory and Records Department. During this time he also developed an interest in freelance journalism.

In 1933 Ernest Bevin asked him if he would take on the job of editing a monthly magazine about walking and camping published by the Victoria House Printing Company, and at the same time take on the job of Rambling and Open-air Correspondent on the *Daily Herald* (the Trades Union Congress was a major stakeholder). The phrase *"the right to roam"* was created by Tom Stephenson and he used it time and time again.

In June 1935 Tom Stephenson's Features Editor rang him up and said that he wanted him to write an article for the next day's paper. Tom had a letter from two American girls on his desk and they mentioned the Appalachian Trail and asked if there was anything similar in England. Tom sat down and wrote his now famous *'Wanted - A Long Green Trail'* article and thought nothing more about it. However, the idea immediately aroused public interest and a demand that something be done.

In 1938 Tom Stephenson called a conference of open-air organisations, where he outlined the route (see chapter *History of the Pennine Way*).

1948 saw Tom Stephenson become the Secretary of the Ramblers' Association, working in an honorary and voluntary capacity for the first four years, and then paid for the remaining seventeen years until he retired in April 1969.

Another milestone in the creation of the Pennine Way was Tom Stephenson's famous three day walk which began on 21 May 1948. This was widely reported in the press at the time because of who his companions were. His walking party consisted of Dr Hugh Dalton MP (ex-Chancellor of the Exchequer and recently appointed President of the Ramblers' Association), Mr Arthur Blenkinsop MP (Parliamentary Secretary, Ministry of Pensions), Mr Fred Willey MP, Mrs Barbara Castle MP, Captain Julian Snow (Lord Commissioner of the Treasury), Mr George Chetwynd MP and Mr Geoffrey de Freitas MP (Under Secretary of State for Air).

The three day walk started at Middleton-in-Teesdale, and on the first day the group walked along the River Tees and Langdon Beck, then via Birkdale to High Cup Nick and down to Dufton. On the second day they walked over Cross Fell, and were met by a party of ramblers from the Darlington HF and CHA Rambling Club, before walking on to Garrigill. On their final day, they continued on to the Roman Wall and followed it eastwards to Housesteads. The walk was Hugh Dalton's suggestion as he wanted to walk part of the Pennine Way, but Tom used the walk to promote his own agenda – the creation of the Pennine Way itself. At the end of the walk, Hugh Dalton said that he was for the creation of the Pennine Way, and that his good friend, Tom Stephenson, who proposed the Way in 1935, thirteen years previously, had waited long enough for it. Nobody at the time realised just how much longer it would take.

Tom Stephenson was one of the first members of the National Parks Commission, which was established by the National Parks Act of 1949. During his time on the Commission, from 1949 until 1953, he proposed that the Peak District became the first of the National Parks, and that the Cheviots be included in the Northumberland National Park. He was made Chairman of the Long Distance Routes Sub Committee and played a prominent part in negotiating with Local Authorities and land owners in obtaining the new rights of way for the Pennine Way, and other long distance routes that were under consideration at the time.

On 16 July 1951, Hugh Dalton MP, now Minister of Local Government and Planning, approved the creation of the Pennine Way and expressed the hope that it would be completed by Easter 1952. It was not in fact finalised until 1964 and the Pennine Way was not officially opened until 24 April 1965.

Tom Stephenson died on 28 February 1987 and in his will, written in 1982, he had this to say:

"From time to time there have been suggestions that there should be a memorial on the Pennine Way or some other method of commemorating my work in connection with that Way. I DESIRE to place on record the fact that any such memorial would be entirely contrary to my wishes and I EXPRESSLY DESIRE that The Ramblers' Association will oppose any proposal for such memorial or commemoration of any kind whatsoever".

When I was Secretary of the Pennine Way Council (PWC), I was fortunate enough to meet Tom Stephenson on 22 June 1985. Tom at that time was the PWC President, and though in his 92nd year, he attended the PWC celebrations held to mark the 50th anniversary of his original article, and the 20th anniversary of the opening of the Pennine Way. At the rally on Malham Lings, Tom spoke to an audience of about 300 people, rewarding them with a rare personal insight into the struggle to achieve *his* Pennine Way.

The idea of the Pennine Way was the invention of one man, Tom Stephenson. It took, however, a committee and many years of hard work to put his idea onto the statute books and Ordnance Survey (OS) maps.

History of the Pennine Way

Three key documents, in my opinion, stand out head and shoulders above the rest, when it comes to the history of the Pennine Way:

1. Tom Stephenson's article of 1935 - *'Wanted – A Long Green Trail'*.
2. The 1938 Pennine Way Conference.
3. A memorandum submitted by the Pennine Way Association to the Scott Committee, which was set up in 1941.

The significance of these is such that they deserve to be fully reported here.

1. *'Wanted – A Long Green Trail'*

The first document is Tom Stephenson's original article, *'Wanted – A Long Green Trail'*, published on 22 June 1935 in the *Daily Herald*, which sowed the seed for a Pennine Way.

The history of this article has been touched on in the previous section on Tom Stephenson. It is now well known that two American girls wrote to Tom Stephenson when he was the Rambling and Open-air Correspondent on the *Daily Herald*. They were going to be visiting England and wondered if we had a footpath similar to the Appalachian Trail, in America, which was 2,000 miles long. Of course at that time there were no long distance footpaths. This was pre-war Britain and wealthy landowners aggressively guarded their grouse moors with gamekeepers. Tom pointed out that Britain had gone backwards when it came to footpaths. Many footpaths had been lost to walkers during the previous century. The Romans built many fine roads across Britain but a lot of these had been swallowed up beneath new roads, cultivated land, or under urban developments. Many old pack horse trails had also disappeared. Tom Stephenson's vision was for some of these to be connected up to form a single long distance "Pennine

Trail". This would protect those individual footpaths and prevent them from being deliberately closed as many others had been in the past.

Tom, a keen walker was aware that there was strong support for the Access to Mountains Bill, particularly by ramblers in the Peak District where opposition by landowners had kept those grouse moors free of any footpath. He hated the signs with "Trespassers will be Prosecuted" that kept walkers from the hills. He called them "wooden liars". It is no coincidence that his proposed Pennine Way would start at Edale, at the foot of the Kinder Plateau. His cry of a "Pennine Way from the Peak to the Cheviots" was taken up by the Pennine Way Conference three years later.

Considering Tom has said that he hastily produced the article, it contained a surprisingly accurate route for the Pennine Way as it is now. As it was King George's Jubilee year he suggested that the path could be called the Jubilee Way, or the Georgian Path. It is a powerful article and well worth reading if you want to track it down. It can be found on the internet if you search for it by its title in Google Images. I am fortunate to have a copy of the original article and surprisingly the copies available on the Internet (and in one guidebook) are missing a couple of sentences. As these relate to a plea to the Trustees of the King George Jubilee to consider providing the funds to establish the route, little is perhaps lost by their omission.

2. The Pennine Way Conference
The second set of two documents comes from the Pennine Way Conference which took place in February 1938. Replicated here is the letter of invitation sent out by Tom Stephenson, followed immediately by the full set of minutes for the conference (including one typing error). Please don't switch off and skip this important piece of history, as these papers are a real eye-opener and, as far as I am aware, have not been reprinted in any other Pennine Way guidebook to date.

PENNINE WAY CONFERENCE

Clapham Common,
London, S.W.4.
31st January, 1938

Dear

A conference to consider the possibility of establishing a Pennine Way from the Peak to the Cheviots will be held at the W.T.A. Guest House, Birchfield, Hope, Derbyshire, on Saturday and Sunday, February 26th and 27th, 1938.

Ramblers' Federations, Y.H.A. groups and kindred associations are being invited to send delegates to this conference and it is hoped your society will be represented.

The proposal for a Pennine Way was first put forward in 1935 and since then it has been under consideration by the Ramblers' Association. Briefly the idea is to establish a continuous right of way along the full length of the Pennines giving the rambler facilities for roaming from Derbyshire to the Scottish Border. Such a route would link the scenic beauties and features of interest in that fine stretch of country and provide an unbroken trail which could be followed without hindrance or any possibility of trouble with gamekeepers or landowners.

It is not suggested that the Pennine Way should be regarded as an alternative to complete "Access to Mountains", nor that it should lessen the demand for that full measure of freedom. Among the keenest supporters of the Pennine Way are some of the staunchest advocates of Access to Mountains and they believe that the attainment of the lesser scheme may well prove a useful step towards the realisation of the greater measure.

At this conference the scheme will be explained in detail and a map of a possible route exhibited. Some of the difficulties to be faced will be indicated and proposals made for a working programme. Criticisms and suggestions will be invited and opportunity given for full discussion.

As a result of the conference it is hoped that a working committee will be appointed to arrange for a survey of the ground, and to take such steps as may be considered necessary for the completion of the scheme at an early date.

The idea of a Pennine Way was first advocated in the Daily Herald and that paper has made a grant to provide hospitality for the weekend for one delegate from each organisation invited. Other representatives of your society who are able to help, may attend at their own expense provided details are sent on the accompanying form together with the appropriate remittance.

The undersigned are convinced that the Pennine Way is a practicable proposal and one worthy of the support of all ramblers, and it is hoped that your society will give the matter consideration and arrange for one or more representatives to attend the Conference.

T. Arthur Leonard
George R. Mitchell
Edwin Royce
Tom Stephenson

PENNINE WAY CONFERENCE
held at W. T. A. Guest House, Birchfield, Hope, Derbyshire
February 26-27, 1938

Present:

T. Arthur Leonard, G. R. Mitchell, E. R. Royce, Tom Stephenson, Mrs.
H. Beaufoy (Convenors and Secretarial)

Blackburn Rambling Association	Chas. Brothers
Co-operative Holidays Association	J. J. Mills
Holiday Fellowship	J. Henderson
Manchester Ramblers' Federation	E. E. Ambler
Manchester Regional Group Y.H.A.	P. G. Furnell
do.	S. R. Smale
North-East Lancs. District Fed. R.A.	Leslie Mills
Peak District & Northern Counties	T. Boulger
Footpaths Preservation Soc.	Harold Wild
do.	B. Gill
do.	G. C. Gradwell
do.	A. W. Hewitt
Pennine Paths Pres. Society	R. Harrison
do.	F. Boocock
Sheffield & District R.F.	Stephen E. Morton
do.	G. H. B. Ward
West Riding R.F.	A. J. M. Sclater
do.	Miss G. Somers
West Riding Y.H.A.	David W. Shaw
Workers' Travel Association	J. E. B. Wright
W.T.A. Mountain Group,	W. Allan Marsden
Northern Section	
Stanley Baron	

MR. T. A. LEONARD who presided said that he had always been interested in the idea of a Pennine Way, first suggested by Mr. Stephenson

two years ago, and he was glad to encourage a scheme, which would be the means of making the public realise the tremendous value of walking. He felt that the Pennine Way would be a wonderful thing to work for and he hoped that the Conference would get down to the practical details, consider the difficulties and ways and means of overcoming them.

MR. TOM STEPHENSON, who followed, said that Mr. Leonard more than anyone else had kept the Pennine Way idea going. The Ramblers' Association had been considering the subject for two years and Mr. Royce and he had been endeavouring to get the route mapped out. They wanted to create a continuous footpath from Kinder Scout to the Cheviots and as far as possible to make it a high level trail linking up places of natural beauty or historical or romantic interest. The suggested route had been planned on these lines. The Pennine Way was not a press stunt but a serious suggestion which it was hoped would be useful to the rambling movement. Neither was it intended that the Pennine Way should detract from the agitation for Access to Mountains. The convenors of the Conference were anxious to obtain complete access to the hills, and were prepared to go on fighting for that ideal. But whilst continuing that agitation, something could perhaps be obtained in the meantime. A Pennine Way would introduce more people to the hills and not all of them would be content to follow a defined path. Such people would increase the demand for complete access. The idea of such a continuous path moreover would have a greater appeal for the general public than what was, after all, a vague notion of access to mountains. If we can create a public opinion believing it is indefensible to withhold a few miles of footpath from the people we shall have made some advance. There would be many difficulties to overcome and much hard work to be done. Of the 250 miles, 68 miles were over ground at present not covered by any track or right of way. Of that 68 miles, 16 miles were over country not at present restricted, leaving approximately 50 miles of new paths to be secured. The first task would be to undertake a survey of the route. As this went on we might find friends prepared to give assistance. When the land had been surveyed maps would be marked indicating meadow land, pastureland, moorland, etc. and a record would be compiled of the owners and the possibilities of obtaining dedication of paths. When this had been done efforts would have to be made to rouse the interest of the public and of individuals and organisations able to help.

1" maps of the route were placed before the Conference and Mr. Royce gave a survey of a possible line for the Pennine Way. From the Peak to the Cheviots the Pennine Way would link the following points: Blackstone Edge, Widdop Cross, Wycoller, Malham (for Gordale), Fountains Fell, Penyghent, Horton in Ribblesdale, Ling Gill, Hawes, Hardraw Force, Keld, Tan Hill, Middleton in Teesdale, High Force, Cauldron Snout, High Cup Nick, Cross Fell, Alston, Maiden Way, Gilsland, Hadrian's Wall, Housesteads, Bellingham, High Rochester, Dere Street, Chew Green Camp, Attonburn Youth Hostel, The Cheviot, and Wooler.

There were two exceptionally difficult areas - one the Peak District, with its well known policy of keeping the town dweller in the town; and the Cheviots, with long distances between possible places of accommodation. Of the 50 miles of new path required, more than 30 were in the neighbourhood of the Peak. Two other districts presented minor difficulties - the industrial region about Blackstone Edge, and another north of Wyecoller where there is the Aire Gap in the Pennines and where we have to come down from our proud aim of a high level track.

Mr. Royce read a letter from Mr. A. Smith of Manchester Ramblers' Federation who was unable to attend. In conclusion, he endorsed Mr. Stephenson's remarks about the Access to Mountains Bill. He was not going to relax his efforts for Access to Mountains and if we could establish something like the Pennine Way and could get people using it, it would stimulate a desire for walking in other parts. And with that in mind he was fully in support of this project.

In the general discussion which followed the following points were raised:

MR. BOULGER asked if dedication of a right of way would be the only aim or whether, where necessary, sufferance rights would be acceptable. Where these were not obtainable it would mean creating a fund to establish a right of way, and it would be advisable to consider taking the route in such cases through the areas of local authorities likely to be sympathetic.

THE CHAIRMAN replied that where it was impossible to obtain dedication it might be advisable to seek sufferance rights, but this would be a matter for the committee.

MR. MARSDEN was of the opinion that sufferance rights would involve legal difficulties. He suggested sectional committees should sift the information, discover sympathetic landowners and endeavour to secure rights of way permanently or for a nominal consideration.

MR. SCLATER said the first thing to do was to get a general idea of the Way, and see how much could be diverted to existing paths. It would be difficult to get local authorities to take steps to create new footpaths, but we should press those authorities to insist on acknowledgement of existing rights of way.

MR. HEWITT said the aim should be to achieve the Pennine Way as early as possible and to adjust it later if better routes could be found.

In reply to MR. SMALE, Mr. Stephenson said that the question of accommodation would have to be considered especially in the Cheviots between Bellingham and Attonburn and the Y.H.A. would of course be approached.

MR. ROYCE added that other accommodation besides Youth Hostels would need to be considered.

MR. WILD thought it unwise to lay down a definite route. The erection of direction posts and provision of stiles would have to be considered and efforts should be made to ascertain which was common land and steps should be taken to search old enclosure awards for existing rights of way and he instanced such awards at Malham.

MR. WARD said an advantage of the Pennine Way would be that it would achieve something of public interest and attract the young people and those not conversant with our problems. The first essential of a Pennine Way was that it should be more or less direct between Derbyshire and the Cheviots and would only deviate according to circumstances met with during the survey. We had to decide whether we were in favour of the Pennine Way as a principle, having regard to Access to Mountains. He wanted complete access but was aware of existing apathy and anything that could be done to awaken interest should be attempted. He and the Sheffield Federation were prepared to oppose the extremists who in regard to access stood for "all or nowt".

MR. BROTHERS said that the Pennine Way should not be regarded as part of the campaign for Access to Mountains. He thought it possible to obtain the Pennine Way and we should endeavour to achieve it without delay.

MR. WARD asked if any approach had been made to the Y.H.A. or the National Council for Physical Fitness. Mr. Stephenson said the Y.H.A. was interested but it was thought advisable to produce a working plan before approaching any public bodies.

MR. MORTON suggested the Board of Education might be approached.

It was then moved by MR. WARD, seconded by MR. AMBLER and carried unanimously:

"That we proceed with the creation of an organisation to establish the Pennine Way without prejudice to the principal of Access to Mountains or similar legislation".

The Conference adjourned at 7.30 p.m. for dinner.

.....

The evening session was spent in detailed consideration of the proposed route and many useful suggestions were recorded for consideration by the committee.

Difficulties in the Peak District were discussed and there were differences of opinion as to the practicability of obtaining new paths. Peak District and Northern Counties Footpaths Preservation Society delegates felt it would be better to decide on deviation.

MR. WARD said we the should not give way before we had begun, and other delegates felt that if we gave in on points like this without fighting, landowners in other districts would argue that if we deviated in the Peak why not on other parts of the route, and we would thus be getting away from the ideal of the Pennine Way.

MR. BARON suggested that as the first part of the route might prove a difficulty, why not commence the Pennine Way a little further north, and indicate possible routes to the Pennine Way, at the same time fighting for the required route. Otherwise it would be putting a weapon into the hands of the landowner.

MR. WARD moved that the question of an alternative route from Kinder to Blackstone Edge be deferred until the reports from other sections had been received. MR. HEWITT seconded and this was carried.

Conference adjourned 10.30 p.m.

.....

Sunday, February 27

MR. LEONARD took the chair at 9.30 a.m. A telegram was read from A. Creech Jones, M. P., regretting inability to attend and wishing the Conference success. Mr. J. Henderson of the Holiday Fellowship and four members of the Sutton in Ashfield Rambling Club were welcomed by the Chairman.

Further consideration was given to the proposed line of the route and Messrs. Royce and Stephenson gave reasons for choice of particular sections.

Waymarking. After general discussion MR. MITCHELL moved that this meeting approves the necessity of some simple form of waymarking of a minimum character being considered by committees. MR. MORTON seconded and this was carried.

The following resolution was moved by MR. MITCHELL, seconded by MR. MORTON:

"That this Conference of representatives of Ramblers' Federations, Regional Groups of the Y. H. A., Footpath Preservation Societies and other organisations interested in Rambling, having considered the desirability of establishing a continuous footway along the Pennines from the Peak to the Cheviots, is convinced that it is in the national interest, on the grounds of the physical and spiritual well-being of the Youth of Britain, that immediate steps towards the creation of such a way should be taken.

Further, this Conference agrees that the wide health-giving moorlands and high places of solitude, the features of natural beauty and the places of historical interest along the Pennine Way, give this route a special character and attractiveness which should be available for all time as a national heritage of the youth of this country and of all who feel the call of the hills and lonely places.

"It is also resolved that a committee representing these organisations shall be appointed and that this committee shall have the power to co-opt such other persons as may be able to assist in furthering the scheme".

"The Committee shall be instructed to arrange for a survey of the Pennines, and to prepare a map indicating (a) existing paths, (b) areas which, although without rights of way, may be traversed, without interference, (c) land from which walkers are at present prohibited.

"Particulars shall be obtained of landowners concerned and data gathered for the purpose of approach and negotiation".

"The Committee shall also be instructed to take any steps considered necessary for the furtherance of the scheme and to secure its adoption at the earliest possible date".

THE CHAIRMAN suggested that a general committee should be appointed and that sub-committees be formed to work out the details in each section as quickly as possible. It was resolved that Mr. E. R. Royce, and Mr. Tom Stephenson be appointed Joint Secretaries with Mrs. H. Beaufoy as Assistant Secretary, and that a committee of six members be elected.   The following were appointed: F. Boocock, C. Brothers, J.J. Mills, S.E. Morton, A.J.M. Sclater, & G.H.B. Ward.

Finance. The question of finance was discussed. MR. WRIGHT suggested that as several national bodies were represented it should be possible to create a fund from these associations. It was then stated that at the moment all that was required was a small fund to cover working expenses. Unknown to the convenors a list was thereupon passed round and it was announced that the sum of £12.10.0 had been promised.

MR MORTON proposed a vote of thanks to the chairman and convenors of the Conference, to Mrs. H. Beaufoy for secretarial assistance, to the W.T.A. for the allowance of special terms for accommodation, to the host and hostess of the guest-house for their services, and to the Daily Herald for a grant for hospitality.   MR. MITCHELL seconded and this was carried unanimously.

MR. STEPHENSON and THE CHAIRMAN responded and the conference concluded at 1 p.m.

The Committee met at 2.15 p.m. It was unanimously agreed that Mr. T. Boulger be co-opted to the Committee. It was decided that the Pennine Way should be divided into the following areas, and the organisations named should be asked to undertake the survey.

1. Peak-Blackstone Edge, Todmorden.

    To be covered by Peak & N.C.C. F.P.S., Manchester R. F., Sheffield R.F., and Manchester Y.H.A.

2. Todmorden-Malham

    N.E. Lancs R.F. and Pennine Paths Preservation Society.

3. Malham - Teesdale, High Cup Nick, Dufton

    West Riding R.F., West Riding Y.H.A.

4. Dufton - Alston

    Dr. W. Goodchild to be invited to co-operate.

5. Alston - Gilsland

    Enquiries to be made of Carlisle H.F. Group.

6. Gilsland - Bellingham

    Enquiries to be made in Newcastle area for possible assistance.

7. Bellingham - Cheviot

    Enquiries to be made in Newcastle area for possible assistance.

......

8.3.38.

3. Memorandum submitted to the Scott Committee

As a result of the Pennine Way Conference, the Pennine Way Association was set up with local sub-committees which immediately began the task of surveying the route and collecting useful data. However the outbreak of the war in 1939 called a halt to the pursuit in detail of such objectives, but during the war years, the Pennine Way Association, along with its associate organisations was able to present a memorandum, to the Scott Committee on Land Utilisation by Rural Affairs.

"The suggestion for a Pennine Way, a continuous foot path from Edale, Derbyshire, along the Pennines, and over the Cheviots to Wooler in Northumberland, was first made in 1935. Considerable interest was created throughout the country by the suggestion and the Ramblers' Association decided it was worthy of examination.

In 1938 the Pennine Way Association was founded at a conference of the Ramblers Association, Youth Hostels Association, Regional Groups, Footpaths Preservation Socs., the Co-op. Holiday Assn., the Holiday Fellowship, the Workers' Travel Association, and other open-air organisations. The conference unanimously agreed that a Pennine Way was desirable "in the national interest on the grounds of the physical and spiritual well-being of the youth of Britain".

It was also agreed that "the wide, health-giving moorlands and high places of solitude, the features of natural beauty, and the places of historical interest along the Pennine Way give this route a special character and attractiveness which should be available for all time as a national heritage of the youth of the country and of all who feel the call of the hills and lonely places". The conference was fully and widely reported in the Press, and the scheme received remarkable publicity.

Reference to the Pennine Way has already been made in memoranda submitted to the Land Utilisation Committee by the

Commons, Open Spaces, and Footpaths Preservation Society, the Ramblers' Association and the Youth Hostels Association.

Here it will probably suffice to mention a few points indicating the general line of the route.

From the head of Edale it is suggested that the Pennine Way should cross Kinder Scout to the Snake Inn and thence to the Derwent Valley and over Bleaklow. Laddow Rocks, Greenfield and Blackstone Edge are on the route to the crossing of the Calder Valley near Todmorden. By Wycoller and the fringe of the Bronte country the way would continue, crossing the Aire Gap near Skipton and reaching the head of Airedale at Malham.

By Fountains Fell and Penyghent the way would lead to Horton in Ribblesdale and then by Ling Gill and an old packhorse road to Hawes in Wensleydale. From Hardraw in the same dale the way would be over Great Shunner Fell to Swaledale, and up that dale to Keld and Tan Hill.

The Stainmoor Gap in the Pennines would be traversed en route for Middleton-in-Teesdale. Thence the Tees would be followed by High Force to Cauldron Snout. The line would then run westwards by Birkdale and up the valley of the Maize Beck to High Cup Nick, and then descend to the village of Dufton.

Cross Fell, the highest point of the Pennines, would be climbed on the way to Garrigill and the South Tyne Valley. From Alston the Maiden Way would lead to Gilsland. Eastward the line of the Roman Wall would be followed to Housesteads.

Next the way would continue to the North Tyne at Bellingham and then to High Rochester in Redesdale. Northward the Roman Road, Dere Street, would lead to the Roman Camps at Chew Green, at the head of coquetdale. Finally the route would run by way of Cheviot to Wooler, Northumberland.

As planned the Pennine Way is approximately 250 miles in length. It does not seek the shortest distance between the two terminal points, but crosses first to one and then to the other side of the Pennines to link up numerous features of scenic or historic interest. In some of the wilder parts of the country, particularly in the northern section, the scarcity of lodging accommodation is a determining factor.

As far as is practicable the route is planned to use existing rights of way other than metalled roads. The desired ideal is a continuous footpath with complete elimination of road walking. By a footpath is meant nothing more than a way trodden out by walkers, and not any artificially surfaced path which would be as undesirable as a metalled road.

From the formation of the Pennine Way Association until the outbreak of war local sub-committees of voluntary workers were surveying the route, and a large amount of useful data had been collected when wartime conditions made it impossible to continue. The information so obtained would be available for use by any authority interested in furthering the scheme.

The above mentioned survey has revealed that of the 250 miles of the route a little less than seventy miles are without footpaths of any kind. Sixteen of the seventy miles are in country where in the past there has been no restriction on rambling. Such liberty, however, might be lost in the future owing to various causes such as change of ownership, development of new grouse moors, or as a consequence of increased usage of the country by walkers. Therefore, it may be said, seventy miles of new footpaths are required to complete the scheme.

Some indication of the route would probably be necessary. Waymarking is a controversial subject, and it may be mentioned the Pennine Way Association does not favour the idea of marking the way with splashes of paint as was the pre-war practice in some continental countries.

On the higher ground stone cairns could be erected as is done in the Lake District, Snowdonia, and other mountainous parts of Britain. These are effective in use, and, being built of stone gathered on the ground, are not out of harmony with the surroundings and need not be unsightly. In the dales it might be necessary in some places to erect some kind of signpost which should be designed to be as simple and inoffensive as is practicable.

A small number of simple footbridges might be required over some of the moorland streams. These need be nothing more elaborate than a single plank adequately secured against flood waters. In many places on the fells dry stone walls are common. However careful one may be, it is not always possible to scale these without dislodging some stones. To avoid this annoyance to the farmer wooden ladder stiles could be erected where required.

In different parts of the country under consideration different means may be used to secure the desired ends.

Thus the creation of National Parks in the Pennines might open large tracts of country at present closed to the public. Elsewhere an effective Access to Mountains Act would provide similar freedom.

Where the route runs over common land the object might be achieved if section 193 of the Law of Property Act, 1925 were made applicable to all commons not already protected, on the lines suggested in the memorandum submitted by the Commons, Open Spaces and Footpaths Preservation Society. Again it might be possible by planning legislation to provide for the creation of long, through walking routes such as the Pennine Way.

Along some sections of the route, land may be acquired by the Forestry Commission which, in other parts of the country, has been sympathetic to the claims of walkers. In other places public-spirited landowners may be prepared to dedicate the required rights of way.

The Pennine Way Association does not wish to impede in any way the agricultural pursuits of the countryside, and it does not believe that the establishment of the Pennine Way would have any injurious effects on rural economy.

In the Lake District and North Wales where more people walk on the hills than in other parts of Britain, one hears very few complaints from the local people who have learned that holiday visitors are a useful source of additional revenue.

Along many parts of the Pennine Way there was in pre-war days already considerable tourist traffic, and many of the small farmers and cottagers were augmenting their incomes by catering for wayfarers.

Where the route crosses the meadowland in the dales there is little difficulty, for it is generally possible to utilise existing rights of way. The trackless portions are on the higher land which consists of rough pasturage, heather and, in places, of large expanses of peat and bog, where there could be little possibility of hindering any agricultural work.

The only serious opposition to the project likely to be encountered would be that from the owners and tenants of the grouse moors.

It was mentioned above that the total length of pathless sections is seventy miles and that sixteen of those miles were in country where there is no restriction on ramblers. Of the remaining fifty odd miles more than thirty miles are at the southern end of the route, in the Peak District of Derbyshire. That area has long been notorious for its lack of public access to the moors, and for the way the hills have been strictly guarded by gamekeepers who, in a number of well-authenticated instances have resorted to violence and other deplorable methods in carrying out what they consider to be their duties.

These restrictions, it is claimed, are necessary for the successful rearing of grouse, but there is evidence that on the moors to which the public have been given access, yield of birds has not suffered. Despite the difficulties, it is well known that many ramblers succeed in evading the gamekeepers and in crossing these forbidden moors. It might be suggested that owners of the grouse moors would find it to be in their own interests to concede a few miles of footpaths which would reduce the necessity for constant watching over a wide area by a large number of gamekeepers.

Before the war the development of motor traffic had made the roads and even the country lanes unsafe and unsuitable for the pedestrian. On them he could find neither pleasure nor comfort and little, if any, opportunity for enjoyment of the peace of the countryside. Instead of providing, at great expense, footpaths alongside these busy thoroughfares, as was often suggested, it would be far more satisfactory to the users to make footpaths away from the highways. Some of these paths need only be of local extent, but provision should be made for long, cross-country routes such as the Pennine Way. There could be little objection to this on the grounds of expense, for the total cost of establishing the Pennine Way would probably be less than the expenditure on the construction of a few yards of a modern motor road.

The popularity of rambling was spreading rapidly before the war, and, in the neighbourhood of the large industrial areas there was urgent need for greater access to the wilder and less cultivated parts of the countryside. It was, in fact, a strange anomaly that the walker had more freedom in the truly agricultural areas than on some barren, uncultivated moorlands. Nowhere was the need for access more pressing than in the Peak District of Derbyshire. There, within easy reach of a great industrial population, was an area of some 200 square miles of moorland to which the public were denied access. Within that area there were only twelve footpaths across the moors exceeding two miles in length.

Kinder Scout, a peaty, moorland plateau of thirteen square miles, was without a single footpath, as was the Bleaklow massif of 37 square miles. Both of these areas are on the line of the Pennine Way. Year after year, the Manchester and Sheffield Ramblers' Federations held demonstrations in the Winnats gorge near Castleton. Those meetings were attended by several thousands of ramblers and resolutions were passed calling for access to the surrounding moorlands and other mountainous parts of Britain. But public feeling was not always voiced so harmlessly, and there were occasions when ramblers came to blows with gamekeepers and policemen. In 1932 a "mass trespass" on Kinder Scout was arranged. This was not supported by the Ramblers' Federations, but more than 400 people gathered at Hayfield, to join in the demonstration. The trespassers did not reach their goal, for some of them came into conflict with gamekeepers, and the police made a number of arrests. The outcome was that at the Derby Assizes, five young men were sentenced to terms of imprisonment varying from two to six months. Without necessarily agreeing with demonstrations of this kind, it may be argued that their occurrence is indication of widely and strongly held grievances.

There are good reasons for believing that after the war rambling will be still more popular, and it will be very regrettable if young people seeking harmless exercise find themselves barred from the wild and lonely places. The discontent and resentment likely to arise from such a state of affairs could, we believe, be avoided by the adoption of the Pennine Way and other schemes of similar character. The Pennine Way would meet a very real need and be a boon to thousands of young people, and an encouragement to them to learn in the best possible way something of the geography and history and varied beauty of their native land. It would provide an escape to lonely heights and refreshing solitudes for many condemned to spend their working lives in mean cities and ugly towns.

We believe, in the words of C. E. Montague, that "At least for some eager and absorbed hours your true rambler has washed away all that futilitarianism out of his soul and has started life again in a heaven of simple effort and clear aim; a career in life opens before him at breakfast; success in life warms him at bedtime. He has discovered a way of playing from which most ways of work have something to learn - concentration and joy and the sense of an absolute value in any hand's turn that is done with a will".

For the reasons we have sought to express we trust the Pennine Way will be included in any post-war planning of the countryside.

Footnote: The Scott Report recommended (para.176) "The recognition of such schemes for main 'hikers' highways' as the proposed Pennine Way but the opening of such paths should not give right of passage over adjoining property". [The Scott Report August 1942 Cmd.6378]

(Note: All attempts have been made to establish any copyright pertaining to the documents reproduced in the above sections 2 and 3, copies of which are held in The National Archives at Kew http://www. nationalarchives.gov.uk.)

Pennine Way signpost outside the Dalesman Café, Gargrave

Featherbed Moss (September 1987) when chestnut palings were used to combat erosion

Archaeological excavations at the unnumbered turret Peel Crags (1987)

Summit of Lamb Hill with early PW signpost (1978)

The original Auchope Refuge Hut (March 1978)

Section 1 – Edale to Crowden

Distance – 16.1 miles / 26 km
Height gained on PW route – 790m (2,592 ft)
Height lost on PW route – 730m (2,395 ft)

Route outline: Edale to Upper Booth; Lee Farm; Jacob's Ladder; Kinder Low; Red Brook; Kinder Downfall; Snake Path; Mill Hill; A57 Snake Pass; Doctor's Gate; Devil's Dike; Alport Low; Bleaklow Head; Wildboar Grain; Clough Edge; Reaps Farm; Torside Reservoir; A628; Crowden.

End of sunken lane with view towards Broadlee-Bank Tor

Probably the best way to arrive at **Edale** is by train. From the railway station you descend, via an underpass, to the road and head northwards up the minor road, passing on the left the Rambler County House Hotel (which used to be called the Rambler Inn and still bears this name above the door), towards the beautiful village church of Grindsbrook. Fieldhead campsite in the grounds of the Peak District

National Park Visitors Centre can be recognised by its multi-coloured, moss-covered roof and the waterfall running over it! Fieldhead is on the way to the Old Nag's Head pub, the 'official start' of the Pennine Way (PW).

Years ago the Pennine Way used to have two routes out of **Edale**. There used to be a 'main route' which left the village by a discrete narrow footpath by the entrance to the (private) driveway to Grindslow House, at the top of the village, down a muddy slope, across a tree trunk lined footbridge, along Grinds Brook and a mild scramble up Grindsbrook Clough onto the Kinder Plateau. Here walkers then headed across peat groughs to Crowden Brook then northwards to the Kinder River, Kinder Gates and **Kinder Downfall**. This required the skill of a map and compass, as it was very easy to get 'misplaced' on the Kinder Plateau. It was a bit like an ant crossing a ploughed field. The alternative, 'bad weather route' followed a more obvious, and circuitous route, via **Jacob's Ladder** and **Kinder Low**. **Edale** was a very popular area in the 1960s and 1970s, especially when there were few long distance paths to test yourself against, and as a consequence there were serious erosion problems on the southern sections of the PW. The main route was less popular with the authorities as the alternative route was easier to maintain. The old route is still a footpath, and you can still walk it, but you won't see any PW signposts on it anymore, which is a shame. I enjoyed the challenge of navigating across Kinder Plateau and there was quite a bit of satisfaction when you reached the **Kinder River** and followed it to **Kinder Downfall**. The bad weather route is now the only PW route and is less of a personal challenge in my opinion, but when you consider that the walk to **Crowden** is about 16 miles away and it has probably the third highest ascent on the whole walk, perhaps, on reflection, this isn't so bad after all!

Section 1.1

Opposite the **Old Nag's Head**, you will see your first of many PW signposts. This one has a yellow chevron (public footpath) on it, a white acorn (long distance path), PENNINE WAY and **Upper Booth** 1¼ miles. It is nice to see some things are still in 'old money'. Cross the road and head towards it. Edale Post Office and General Store and Cooper's Café and Caravan and Campsite will be on your left. The start of the PW takes you west, to a sunken, sometimes muddy, path where holly bushes and ash trees abound. At the end of the sunken path you pass through two small wooden gates quite close together (there is a signpost to the right of the second gate) and out onto open country (see photograph at start of section). Here are the first of many slabs, which will aid your navigation, and speed you towards your overnight accommodation. There are far too many slabs for my liking on the first two days of the walk, but cheer up, they aren't as prolific in the days that follow.

The path contours around **Broadlee-Bank Tor** to your right, passing through several fields in the process, with dry-stone walls with small wooden gates in them. You shouldn't get lost, as the flagstones beneath your feet will guide you. You soon pass a wooden bench on the right, next to the path with a poem on it:

> "*Office bustle for leaves rustle*
> *Mobiles ringing for birds singing*
> *Lover's rejection for water's reflection*
> *Twenty-first century for glimpse of eternity.*"

Descending to **Upper Booth** there is a lovely campsite with a convenient public phone box nearby.

Mobile phone signals can be a bit sporadic on the PW so a call box is great. If your home phone has free evening and weekend calls, ask your partner to ring you back! I usually stay here because it makes for a shorter day to **Crowden** and it is quiet. I usually carry a small lightweight one-man tent and no cooking gear so my overall pack weight is kept low. It also helps avoid the comments from other walkers that I used to get about carrying a mountain on my back. It is surprising how much weight and bulk a stove, fuel, and billycan and cup take up. Accommodation for a solo walker on a limited budget can be quite expensive outside of campsites and youth hostels so if you are trying to keep the cost of your walk down, a lightweight tent, at least for the first few days, is ideal. Crowden youth hostel will be closed to PW walkers as from 1 April 2014 it will be run as an outdoor centre which will only accept large (pre-booked) groups, so you will have to use B&Bs or camp at **Crowden**. A single bed in a B&B generally costs about £10 more than sharing a twin or double. Further north, where there is more plentiful accommodation, an easy option is to post the tent home. A tent also enables you to get an early start in the morning and avoids lengthy detours off the route to your accommodation. If you take muesli for breakfast, there is no cooking time and washing up is easy.

Section 1.2

You leave Upper Booth by the phone box and another PW signpost, where you turn right (NW) along a minor tarmac road, which takes you to **Lee House**. Here the tarmac road becomes a track. By the information shelter is a stone bench, which has the words 'Jacob's Ladder, Edale Cross, Kinder Downfall', carved around the edges of it. Here you go through a gate and continuing in the same direction, you follow the track, which takes you to a gate in front of an old packhorse bridge and the start of **Jacob's Ladder** (named after Jacob Marshall, a 'Jagger' who sent his packhorses up the zigzag while he took a more direct route to the top). At the top of the hill you will find a cairn and a Peak District & Northern Counties Footpaths Preservation

Society signpost (these are metal and painted green with white wording – this one has No 85 and 1939 on it) or you can follow the route the packhorses used to take and follow the stone stepped zigzag up, which is longer but not as steep. At the top you follow a wide path, which takes you in a westerly direction. You leave the path when a relatively new (2011) slabbed path appears on the right and you follow this. This cuts off a corner in the 'old' route.

If you want to visit Edale Cross, which is a few minutes off the PW route, don't take the slabbed path to the right but continue straight ahead until you come to a cross track with a wooden gate across the path, with a PW signpost directing you right, up the slope towards **Edale Rocks**. Ahead, through the gate, about five minutes away, is Edale Cross, which is medieval (to the left of the wooden gate is a path to Brown Knoll). If you decide to visit Edale Cross, retrace your steps back to the gate and PW signpost and walk up the sloped path to rejoin the PW, which is slabbed.

Section 1.3

After a short while the slabs swing northwards by a large cairn and here you ascend left towards **Edale Rocks**. On a clear day, navigation isn't a problem here, but quite frequently there is mist about and care must be taken to avoid missing the correct path. If you do miss this turn off, you will end up at Edale Head and you will have to retrace your steps back to the large cairn. Once you reach **Edale Rocks**, the PW is more straightforward. You continue slightly west of north until you reach the trig point at **Kinder Low** (S 4113). Here the PW is poorly defined and descends in roughly the same direction (NNW). After a short while you reach the edges, which you follow northwards (NNE) to **Red Brook**. From here you continue following the edges to **Kinder Downfall**.

Shortly before you reach **Kinder Downfall**, look out for a faint path, which appears on the left. This path takes you to a good photo point for the Downfall, but take care here as it also takes you quite close to the edge. After you have taken your photograph(s), retrace your steps and continue along the edges to the Downfall.

Section 1.4

Kinder Downfall is a good place for a rest, so cross the river and take off your boots and socks and let your feet breathe for a quarter of an hour while you have a drink and a snack. If the weather is clear you will be able to see Kinder Reservoir to the west.

Feet, mind and body suitably refreshed, the path ahead lies slightly west of NW, still on the edges. You are now on a sometimes sandy and sometimes stony path. The only feature between the Downfall and the **Snake Path** is a fence with a large kissing gate in it about half a mile from the Downfall. There is quite a steep descent down to the **Snake Path** on a stone lined path where care is needed.

The 'Snake' comes from the Cavendish coat of arms of the Duke of Devonshire, who once owned large areas of moorland around here, and whose crest includes a serpent.

There is a Peak & Northern Footpaths Society guidepost at the cross-roads at the bottom. Ascend ahead to **Mill Hill** where you will find a sprawling cairn and a stone PW marker directing you to turn right towards **Glead Hill**. Next to the marker is a small post with a Trailblaze box attached to it.

Trailblaze is a recent innovation for runners who want to log their times between sections of the route. There is a charge and a website for the scheme, however, it is just as efficient to use a stopwatch if that is what you want to do. Personally, I believe that the PW is for walkers. There are plenty of other challenges for runners, which don't involve long distance footpaths.

In the early days of the PW, walkers followed a line of posts from **Mill Hill**, (the stumps of some are still visible in the peat pools to the left of the flag stones) over a very glutinous eroded peaty path. I remember one occasion when one of my companions sunk up to his groin in the peat. Now there is a nice firm flagged path, which takes you all the way to the **A57 Snake Pass** on a line mostly to the right of the old route. Much as I dislike slabs, it is a considerable improvement on what was there before and it does speed up your progress. Sometimes the old path was so badly eroded that you had to constantly keep going further to the right and back again looking for firmer ground. This added mileage and time to what is a long 16-mile day.

Section 1.5

Approaching the **Snake Pass** you will be able to see quite a few cars and lorries on it long before you reach it. At the road go through a small gate (acorn sign on the right gatepost) with a National Trust Ashop Moor sign to the road. Cross the road, with care, to another small gate. A PW signpost by a small pond just before the gate informs you that you are 2½ miles from **Mill Hill** and that it is 2¼ miles to **Bleaklow Head**, the last climb of the day. A good sandy path going off into the distance replaces the slabs. Again this is an improvement on what was there in the 1970s when chestnut palings were laid on top of bundles of twigs sunk into the peat (see photograph of Featherbed Moss, September 1987).

After about ⅓ mile you cross **Doctor's Gate**, which has a guidepost with a blue arrow nailed onto it. Continue ahead to **Devil's Dike**, a sunken path with a good sandy track in it. Slabs greet you when you exit it. You now need to keep alert as the path (sometimes slabbed) is signed by a number of stone markers with directional arrows and 'PW' or an acorn carved into them. The path later follows the banks of **Hern Clough** as you ascend NNW towards **Bleaklow Head**. Don't expect to see any views though, as the Clough is in a dip all the way up. There is another stone marker as you leave the Clough. **Bleaklow Head** appears, almost out of nowhere, not long afterwards. It is recognised by a large sprawling triangular shaped cairn with a post in the centre.

There is a deviation from the 'old' PW route, between **Hern Clough** and Bleaklow as the 'old' route used to go via Hern Stones and the Wain Stones ('The Kiss' in Wainwright's *Pennine Way Companion*) but in poor visibility the current route is easier to follow.

Section 1.6

Care should be taken when leaving **Bleaklow Head**. Just before the sprawling cairn is another stone marker with an acorn and a directional arrow pointing half left. This path (the PW) will take you to a fence, which you should follow. After another stone marker you veer west then gradually descend to follow a path above **Wildboar Grain**. After a while the path descends and crosses the stream. As you ascend again, look out for a crude PW and arrow carved into one of the exposed rocks. After a while you reach a wooden step stile, (crossing an extremely short six-bar fence!), with a wire fence on both sides. The path is now above **Torside Clough** (on the right) on **Clough Edge** and is narrow and rocky in places. **Torside Reservoir** soon comes into view. Before a very steep descent to the track at **Reaps Farm**, there is another Peak & Northern Footpaths Society signpost (No 384 2010). At the track (PW signpost) turn left to reach the **B6105**.

If you are camping in **Crowden**, or have made other arrangements around the **A628** ahead, then continue on the PW.

Here you need to think about your overnight accommodation following the loss of Crowden youth hostel on 1 April 2014. There are B&Bs in Glossop who may pick you up from here, or you can walk into Glossop, which is a couple of miles away to the west. A closer option is the Old House B&B, which is located approximately 600 yards left down the road. As accommodation is limited here, it is advisable to book your overnight accommodation in advance.

Section 1.7

Descend to cross the line of an old railway, which is now the Trans Pennine Trail, and descend to the dam at the head of the reservoir. At the other side of the reservoir you ascend up some steps to a small wooden gate (ignore the revolving metal stile on the left of the gate). There is a wooden sign on the wall to the left of the gate (to the right of the stile) with a blue directional marker (PW and Bridleway) to aid navigation. There is also an acorn and various coloured arrows on the gate itself. Follow a clear path uphill through woodland to some steps up to the **A628** (PW signpost with a blue chevron – **Crowden** ½ mile). This can be quite a busy road so take care as you cross it. Turn right for a few yards then left up a tarmac track. This will take you into **Crowden** where there is the Camping & Caravan Club campsite. On the way to the campsite you pass a PW signpost on the left of the track, which has another Trailblaze box on it. This path takes you NNW to **Crowden Great Brook**, which is your route for tomorrow.

Section 2 – Crowden to Standedge

Distance – 10.9 miles / 17.8 km
Height gained on PW route – 670 m (2,198 ft)
Height lost on PW route – 480 m (1,575 ft)

Route outline: Crowden to Laddow Rocks; Dun Hill; Black Hill; A635; Wessenden Head Reservoir; Wessenden Reservoir; Blakely Clough; Black Moss Reservoir; A62 Standedge Cutting.

***PW descending towards Blakely Clough north-west
of Wessenden Reservoir***

Section 2.1

Retrace your steps back from **Crowden** to the PW signpost with the Trailblaze box that you passed yesterday on your way to the campsite. Turn right (NNW) along a good path. Ahead of you are a couple of stiles before you reach a plantation on the right of the path, which was planted in 1980 in memory of Harry Phillips. At first you gradually ascend towards **Laddow Rocks** on a rocky path with ferns close to both sides of the path in the summer. You then descend to cross a small stream (**Crowden Brook**) before ascending again over a knoll, (**Rakes Rocks**), passing a wooden directional marker warning of 'Deep Bogs' if you stray off the route, before descending again to a second stream (**Oakenclough Brook**). From here you have the final ascent to **Laddow Rocks**, crossing a narrow fast stream, which usually provides a good source of water if you are thirsty (use water purifying tablets or a filter if you have any doubts about the purity of the water).

Section 2.2

The path along **Laddow Rocks** is flat and sandy but it can be narrow in places and it goes quite close to the edge on occasions. On sunny days there are great views back along **Crowden Brook**. The path descends to a feeder stream into **Crowden Great Brook**, which can be crossed without wet feet in dry weather. This is a good spot for a boots off break if the weather is good, before the gradual ascent to **Black Hill**. A second feeder stream is crossed, after which you meet the first slabs of the day. The first section of slabs was laid relatively recently (2011) and they soon link with older, more established slabs. This is a great improvement on the 1970s and 80s when the path was on the peat and got very boggy with the passage of thousands of feet. The slab path follows **Crowden Great Brook** on your right and when it meets **Meadowgrain Clough**, it leaves the Clough and heads NE, reaching a stile in a wooden fence (with a dog gate in it). This is another good spot for a break.

As you ascend you will see a tall slender mast ahead. This is Holme Moss and it isn't on the route, but on clear days it is reassuring to see it. You pass **Dun Hill** almost without noticing it and continue to **Black Hill**. This used to be a very bleak place indeed but now it probably should be renamed Green Hill after a considerable amount of regeneration to the summit. The slabs to the trig point on **Black Hill** were a lifesaver when they were first laid. Far better than having to wade through the glutinous peat to reach the only solid ground of **Soldier's Lump** which houses the trig point (S 2958). In the 1970s the white painted trig point was on a mound of peat a couple of feet above the existing peat level. Now a well-built cairn surrounds it.

> The official route off **Black Hill** used to be called the Wessenden Alternative, as the 'main route' used to leave **Black Hill** west-wards to a cairn, then NW over Wessenden Head Moor to meet the **A635** at the Greater Manchester-West Yorkshire boundary, and then over Featherbed Moss, White Moss and on to Black Moss. Various methods were used to avoid the truly dreadful bogs in this area, including long lengths of chestnut palings. Again, the current route, with its slabs, is heaven compared to what walkers had to deal with in the 1980s. On older OS maps the 'main route' from **Black Hill** to the **A635** was shown as 'Pennine Way undefined', and you followed a line of posts over very boggy ground.

Section 2.3

Leaving **Black Hill** is easy as the slabs direct you NNE before you reach an old boundary ditch where the slabs swing NW. On a sunny day you should be able to see the **A635** from here with a line of cars and lorries on it. The way ahead looks flat but there is a slight sting in the tail in the form of **Dean Clough**, where there is a steep stepped descent into the Clough and a stepped ascent out again. Once this is passed, it is an easy walk to the small wooden gate in the fence by the road. The signpost here informs you that **Black Hill** is 1¾ miles behind you and **Wessenden Lodge** is 2 miles ahead. There is a great view of the path you have just walked behind you. On a sunny day Holme Moss, at the end of a long line of slabs, and **Black Hill** to the right of it, are clearly visible.

Section 2.4

Turn right along the road for a short distance until another signpost directs you left down another minor road (the **Wessenden Head Road**) towards Meltham. Be on the lookout for another signpost on the left by a set of metal gates, a larger one for vehicular traffic and smaller one for bikes and pedestrians. To the left of the gate is a small information board (Marsden Moor Heritage Trail), which is worth a read. Go through the gate on the right to a good track, which descends to **Wessenden Head Reservoir**, passed on the left. Continue descending on the track, contouring round **Leyzing Clough** on the right, and again contouring round **Sike Clough**, also on the right. The track continues to descend to **Wessenden Reservoir** and the **Wessenden Lodge**. On the right, next to the path, by the trees, is a new Peak & Northern Footpath Society signpost (No 421 2012). As you walk past the Lodge you may be lucky and see fallow deer in a fenced enclosure above the track. The track crosses a bridge (there is a pretty waterfall on the hillside to your left) and soon meets a PW signpost, (blue chevron pointing back and yellow chevron point-ing left) which directs you down a steep slope to where you cross a stream via a narrow wooden footbridge with a grab rail on the right, and you then scramble up the steep slope on the other side to a covered water tank (a photograph of the signpost can be seen at the beginning of this section). Continue westwards on a narrow path to a weir (**Blakely Clough** on your right). Here you cross over **Blakely Clough** and continue in the same direction with the Clough now on your left. The path is initially peat, then stony, then slabbed with cotton grass on both sides. The slabs take you to **Black Moss Reservoir**, (passing **Swellands Reservoir** on the right), where it bears right (NW) along its eastern shore, then left (SW) just before a fence, along its northern shore. You then pass through a wooden kissing gate (with a dog gate) in a wire fence to meet a good track heading NW again. This track takes you through two more kissing gates to a track just before **Redbrook Reservoir**, where there is an apparently blank stone marker, but if you look on the other side of it, there is 'MH 750 yards' carved into it.

A local National Trust volunteer believes these stones are parish boundary markers with the 'M' standing for Marsden and 'H' for the parish of Huddersfield. Marsden until the 1860s was in two parishes, Huddersfield north of the river Colne and Almondbury to the south. Usually the lettering for modern boundary markers is on the outside looking in, but he thinks that may not have been the custom in the past. There is a second boundary stone at **Haigh Gutter** on the PW (marked 'BS' on the OS maps) and it is believed that this would probably have been placed where the old pack horse route passed from Marsden in Huddersfield to Saddleworth.

An old packhorse trail from Marsden (now part of the Standedge Trail) comes in from the right (east) here. Turn left (west) along the track. A few yards along the track is another of the Peak & Northern Footpaths Society green metal signposts (No 357 2008). The track continues towards the **A62** in the **Standedge Cutting**. Before it reaches the road it bends left again to parallel it. At **Brun Clough Reservoir** the track turns sharp right to descend to the road. The car park here once housed the famous Peter's Transport Café. This was a place of legend in the very early days of the Pennine Way. Alas it burnt down in 1970 and was never replaced. There is an old PW notice board in the car park.

At **Standedge** there is some limited accommodation. Globe Farm used to be the place to go but alas that too has passed into legend. Carriage House is a mile down the cutting on the right (Mount Road) and provides B&B and camping. There is a MetroLine bus stop here, where, on the other side of the road, you can catch a 184 bus into Marsden (see *http://www.wymetro.com/ynb* for details). On the way to the Carriage House you pass the Great Western Inn on the left and Redbrook Reservoir on the right. There is also a unique PW road sign on the right as you carefully make your way there along the grass verge.

If you don't want to rely on buses, when you get to **Wessenden Lodge**, an alternative option is to continue on to Marsden where there are a few B&Bs and shops. After the Lodge you continue down the track (Kirklees Way) instead of descending down the bank to the stream and footbridge. This track will take you into Marsden and you can retrace your steps back to the Lodge the following day.

Section 3 – Standedge to Mankinholes

Distance - 12 miles / 19.5 km (11.4 miles / 18.3 km to Withens Gate)
Height gained on PW route – 320 m (1,050 ft)
Height lost on PW route – 385 m (1,263 ft)

Route outline: Standedge to Millstone Edge; Northern Rotcher; A640; White Hill; M62; Blackstone Edge; White House; Blackstone Edge Reservoir; Head Drain; Light Hazzles Reservoir; Warland Reservoir; Warland Drain; Withens Gate; Mankinholes.

Junction of PW and Oldham Way at Northern Rotcher

Section 3.1

Retrace your steps back to where you left the PW yesterday. NW is your initial direction to take. By the side of the **A62** you should see a PW signpost with **Black Moss** 1 mile, pointing back to where you met the road yesterday, and **A640** 2¼ miles, pointing towards where you are heading today. After a five minute walk uphill, you come to a 3-pointer signpost where you meet the Pennine Bridleway for the first time. You will meet it several more times on your walk. Here the PW and the Oldham Way run together for a couple of miles. Opposite is a small kissing gate in a wire fence, which you go through. You are now at the beginnings of **Millstone Edge**. Before you reach the Edge proper, you will see another signpost with 'Pennine Way North' and 'Pennine Way South' on it. This, as far as I am aware, is the only one of its type on the walk.

Millstone Edge is well named as it is made of millstone grit. The drop on your left slopes away but on a fine day, there are some good views there. Just after the trig point (S 4402), over the slope on the left, is the **Dinner Stone** where there is a memorial to Ammon Wrigley, a local poet.

Ammon Wrigley's ashes were scattered from this spot on 14 September 1946 as were those of his two daughters, Amy (18 May 1957), and Alice (6 July 1965). Also on a rock face close by, is a small plaque remembering Bob Glentworth (1931–1997), who was a former member of the Pennine Way Association, amongst his other interests.

Continuing NW along the edge you should keep an eye open for a small square stone marker which directs you to turn off to the right along a well made narrow path. This takes you to the **A640** and a small stream called **Haigh Gutter**, which is crossed using a small wooden footbridge. There is a Peak & Northern Footpath Society green signpost facing southwards, at the junction of two paths here, just before the road (No 358 2008) with **Standedge** & **Edale** via the Pennine Way on one fork and Marsden via Close Gate Bridge on the other. By the road is a PW signpost with 'Pennine Way (South) **Standedge** 1.8 miles' on it. The first of only two PW signposts with a decimal point on it! On the opposite side of the road is another PW signpost, next to a boundary stone with a rounded top (which makes it resemble a gravestone), with 'MH' carved into it.

Cross over the road and, continuing in the same direction, (NW), walk uphill, meeting a dry stone wall on the left of the path. You cross the summit of **Rape Hill** and descend to a clough, then ascend up the slope on the other side. At the top of the slope is a wooden stile in a fence which marks the boundary of the Marsden Moor Estate. Soon after you meet a white painted trig point (S 4487) with a wireless telegraph mast half right in the distance. The trig point is on **White Hill**. Continue in the same direction, passing through two small gates (with YWS 2010 stencilled on them in blue paint). After the second gate, **Green Hole Hill** is on your left and the path swings NNW, passing a large cairn by a gate in the fence on your right before descending towards the **A672**. Sometimes there is a white refreshment van in the lay-by here but don't depend on it for your morning snack. There should be a large red flag on a bendy pole if the 'chef' is in residence. See it as a bonus if it is there. By the **A672** is another Pennine Way (South) signpost, pointing back with **A640** 1.9 miles on it. You pass a huge WT mast on your left and head northwards on a narrow path to something rather unusual and unique – a purpose built footbridge spanning the **M62** motorway.

Had the PW been created today, it would probably have been routed east along the A672 to junction 22 and back again. In 1965 when it was first opened, the M62 wasn't built and in 1970 when it was, the PW had a very powerful lobby. It is weird being back in 'civilisation' again after a couple of days' peace and quiet. The traffic is very noisy and it can be very windy on the footbridge so hold onto your hat!

Section 3.2

Ascend the obvious track which swings to the left after you cross the footbridge. This path could be clearly seen on your descent to the motorway footbridge. In the early days of the PW, this section of the route was on wet, badly eroded peat with cotton grass very evident. The name **Redmires** (passed on the way up the hill) conjured up all kinds of tales from Pennine Wayfarers. Now this particular beast has been tamed. The track shortly takes you through a gate in a boundary fence, after which it swings NW, passing a low stone-built shelter on your right, and it continues to **Blackstone Edge** where you will encounter the rather unusual sight of a trig point (S 4502) on top of a very large boulder (see photograph in centre spread). This should be painted white but there have been occasions when graffiti artists have been at work covering large areas of it with a black spray can.

At the trig point you continue in the same direction but make sure you don't lose any height at this point to avoid deviating from the PW route. If you keep high, you will shortly come to an old packhorse road on the other side of a wire fence with a wooden step stile in it. Here, directly ahead of you is the **Aiggin Stone**.

> The notice nearby says that this is a medieval guide stone and that it is 600 years old. It has obviously seen some damage as the cross, carved into it, is missing its top. There are also some ancient initials carved into it.

Here at the 'T junction' you turn left and descend the paved 'Roman Road' to meet and cross **Broad Head Drain**, where you turn right (the concrete drain should be on your right now). Continue along next to this drain (it curves around to the left then to the right) until you reach an old quarry. Here you descend, left, to the road (**A58**) where you turn right, up the hill, to **The White House** Free House (pub).

Section 3.3

Just past the pub is the second PW map board on the route (the first was in the car park at **Standedge**). A few yards beyond this, immediately after an old stone bridge over the road, look out for a PW signpost on the left, next to a very unusual metal gate, (there is a pylon opposite on the right), which is the entrance to a very wide, level track. This track contours around **Head Drain**, passing **Blackstone Edge Reservoir**, **Light Hazzles Reservoir** and **Warland Reservoir**. Navigation is easy on this section as the Drain and reservoirs are on your right as you walk along the track. Between **Blackstone Edge Reservoir** and **Light Hazzles Reservoir**, before a disused quarry on the right, there is an interesting arched footbridge (don't cross it, keep to the broad track) which allowed sheep access to both sides of the Drain. Carved into one of the rock faces of the disused quarry is the following poem, entitled 'Rain':

> *'Be glad of these freshwater tears*
> *each pearled droplet some salty old sea bullet*
> *air lifted out of the waves, then laundered and sieved, recast as a*
> *soft bead and returned.*
> *And no matter how much it strafes or sheets it is no mean feat to*
> *catch one raindrop clean in the mouth*
> *to take one drop on the tongue, tasting cloud pollen, grain of the*
> *heavens, raw sky.*
> *Let it teem, up here where the front of the mind distils the brunt*
> *of the world.'*

The next aid to navigation is overhead power lines which you pass under. There is also a PW signpost here and a second signpost (not a PW one) on the right side of the track directing walkers to the White Holme Reservoir Walk. Keep ahead on the Pennine Way. The next signpost that you come to has 'Public Footpath' and an upside down acorn on it. There is a path which descends left away from the track which you should ignore. Some kind soul has drawn PW and an arrow on the post in black to ensure that PW walkers keep ahead, along the side of **Warland Reservoir**. After this last reservoir, you now have a drainage ditch called the **Warland Drain** on your right. You should be able to see **Stoodley Pike** in the distance. Don't get too excited though as you won't visit it until tomorrow.

After a short distance, the Drain turns sharp right, and then curves left. When the Drain curves sharp right again, you leave it at the PW signpost, for a sandy path heading north. This is slabbed in places. The finger post here tells you that **Stoodley Pike** is 1½ miles away. Pass three boundary stones. Your next point of reference is a stone seat set into a very small short dry stone wall. This is dedicated to Cyril Webster, (by his children), a walker who died in December 1992. Shortly afterwards you come to **Withens Gate**, where a causey path (a bit like a slabbed path, but this was here long before the Pennine Way was thought of), descends to the left. This will lead you to **Mankinholes** youth hostel, your overnight stop. Follow this (with care in the wet) down to the corner of a wall. Continue ahead with the wall on your right until you come to some cross tracks. Here a walled lane on the right is met. A signpost by the gate directs you along the lane to **Mankinholes**. As you leave the lane you will see some countryside artwork in the form of stone sheep with metal heads. Continue ahead on a tarmac road (at another signpost), past a series of stone troughs on the right. After several yards, look for a smoke blackened stone building with a prominent YHA logo on the side and a metal gate with 'YHA' in white paint embedded within it by the side of the building. This is the entrance to the youth hostel.

Section 4 – Mankinholes to Ponden

Distance – 14.4 miles / 23.3 km (including 1 km off route to Mankinholes)
Height gained on PW route – 685 m (2,247 ft)
Height lost on PW route – 500 m (1,640 ft)

Route outline: Mankinholes to Withens Gate; Stoodley Pike; Lower Rough Head; Callis Wood; A646; Badger Lane; Colden Water; Colden; Mount Pleasant; Clough Head Hill; Gorple Cottages; Walshaw Dean Lower Reservoir; Walshaw Dean Middle Reservoir; Withins; Upper Heights; Ponden Hall.

Stoodley Pike in the distance looking back southwards

Retrace your steps back to where you left the PW yesterday; come out of the hostel, turn left along the tarmac road, ahead along the walled lane to the gate at the end, turn left up the causey path (with the dry stone wall on your left initially) to **Withens Gate** to regain the ridge.

If for any reason you don't want to climb all the way back up to the ridge, shortly after leaving the hostel, just before you reach the walled lane, there is a signpost for the Pennine Bridleway on the left. This follows a cart track, which is ambitiously named London Road, and it contours around the hillside below the PW and rejoins it after 1¾ miles at a three pointer signpost with a Trailblaze box on it. This is quite a pleasant walk with great views of **Stoodley Pike** ahead on your right as you follow the track. The disadvantage is that you don't get to see the **Stoodley Pike** close up, and of course you miss a small section of the PW.

Section 4.1

Having come up from **Mankinholes** turn left along the ridge, passing a tall leaning stone on your right. Continue ahead along the ridge (there are views of Todmorden to your left) until **Stoodley Pike** is reached (there are 39 steps corkscrewing up inside the monument to a viewing platform. It is very dark inside so you will need a torch if you decide to go in and explore). Shortly after passing **Stoodley Pike**, you descend eastwards to a wooden stile in a wire fence. There is a white acorn on the grab post. After a short walk you reach a wall with a stile in it. From here you descend, first northwards, then NNE to meet a track and the Pennine Bridleway. The signpost here says **Callis Bridge** is 2¾ miles away (the previous signpost on this spot used to say that it was 3 miles away).

Cross the track and follow a wall on your right to a wooden step stile. Cross the stile and continue ahead to the wall corner and cross a field NE on a slabbed path to a kissing gate. Go through the gate. With another wall on your left, continue in the same direction, pass-ing under power lines (twice), then through a kissing gate, to meet a tarmac track by **Lower Rough Head Farm**. Descend on the tarmac track, through a metal gate across the track and past a Pennine Bridleway signpost on the right, until you come to a PW signpost where you descend, via some steps, into the wood, down a slope, to rejoin the track below. This takes you to a bridge over the canal (water treatment works on the right before the bridge). There is also another PW map board here. Cross the bridge and continue to the road (**A646**).

Section 4.2

At the road, cross via the traffic lights and turn right along the pavement. You will shortly see a stone railway bridge on your left (**Underbank Avenue**), which you must pass under. Directly ahead on the other side of the bridge is a steeply ascending cobbled path between two walls, which passes several houses before taking you to a minor road. Turn left at the road until you reach an old churchyard, which originally belonged to the Mount Olive Chapel (now demolished). Here you will see a squat wooden signpost directing you right, to a stile, and a path which ascends NE up an overgrown (in summer) path. Rather unusually, the sign also has a curved arrow directing walkers left if they want to follow the old Wainwright route here (the official route is to the right). At the end of the path you come to a set of steps with iron railings on the right. These take you past a small stone building with a small stream passing underneath it via a culvert (a long drop loo). At the top of the steps, continue on a track uphill to pass a house on your left to a road. Turn left along the road to a T-junction. Here you bear left again for a few yards to a PW signpost on the right.

Leave the road and head NNW passing **Popples Farm** on your left and **Scammerton Farm** on your right, to reach a road (**Badger Lane**). Cross and continue ahead in the same direction up **Pry Hill** with a dry stone wall on your left and a single strand wire fence on your right, shortly passing a wind turbine on the right, parallel with **Badger**

Fields Farm. If you look back, you will see **Stoodley Pike** on the ridge behind you.

At the top of the ridge, if you look ahead, you can see a cluster of white walled houses (a small housing estate) at the top of a large field, with trees on both sides of the field. This is your next objective. If the day is clear you can see the line of the PW ahead, following the left side of a wall which ascends up the other side of the valley to the trees on the right. When it meets the trees on the right, it goes diagonally towards the trees on the left to meet a lane, which will take you to the road.

Descend, (stone wall still on your left), through a small kissing gate, past a small stone ruin on the right, through two more kissing gates, then via a narrow overgrown walled lane to a tarmac lane.

Section 4.3

Cross the lane and go down some steps to an ancient gritstone footbridge over **Colden Water**. This small dell goes under the name of **Hebble Hole**. You will have seen this name on the signpost (see photograph at the beginning of this section) at the tarmac road before **Badger Fields Farm** (at **Badger Lane**), and you will see it on a few more PW signposts as you head northwards. Go up the slope to meet a cross path where you turn right for a few yards before turning left, by a small guidepost with an acorn and yellow directional arrows on it. The PW then takes you up some steps to a gate. Continue ahead (old wall on the right and wire fence on the left), passing under some power lines to reach a wooden step stile with a small red gate set in a wire fence, next to a dry stone wall. Here caution is needed regarding route finding. Bear half left across the field crossing three more stiles to meet a track with grass growing up the middle (leaving two gravel strips where vehicle wheels go). Continue up this, passing a small housing estate on the right, to meet a road with a PW signpost by it (pointing back the way you have just come with '**Hebble Hole** ⅓ ml' on it) and a bus stop on your right. There is another PW signpost on the opposite side of the road directing you to go straight ahead.

If you became 'misplaced' and came to a track to the right of the small housing estate, you will still come to the road but the bus stop will be visible on your left. You will need to turn left, pass the bus stop and look out for the PW signpost on your right.

Continue ahead for a short distance on a gravel path between two wire fences to another road, with a domestic garage on your right. Turn right on the road for about 8 yards, then left up a slope. There is a PW signpost on the road before the slope, pointing you to **Heptonstall Moor**, and a second sign attached to it advertising May's Aladdin's Cave (Highgate Farm Shop where you can buy various supplies that PW walkers usually need. They also provides free camping if you have a tent and can't go any further). Continue ahead up the slope with a wire fence on your left and a small plantation on your right. When the path bends to the left you cross a stile. A broken wall replaces the fence. Ahead you pass **Mount Pleasant Farm** and shortly afterwards go through a small wooden gate (white acorn and directional arrow on the right post) and onto the moor to meet another PW signpost with '**Top Withens** 6¼ miles' on it. Here you bear half left across the heather moorland. If the weather is clear the path will be visible ahead as it heads towards a wall corner. After the wall corner, keep an eye open for an unusual small weather beaten PW finger post beside the path. The path heads NW ascending the side of **Clough Head Hill**. There are slabs here but a walking stick or pole is useful too as one section ends in mud and water. The path swings further left to meet a double set of dry stone walls which take you to a stony track with a three finger signpost for both the PW and Pennine Bridleway which merge here for a short distance.

Section 4.4

Turn right down the track towards a rather grey looking house (**Gorple Cottages**) with four double-glazed windows on each of its two storeys. By the house is a rather unusual pair of iron gates, which you pass through. Here you will see a four-fingered signpost, where again the Pennine Bridleway takes a different path. Follow the PW finger post directing you to **Clough Foot** ahead, to descend into **Graining Water**, down a stony and grassy path. The PW passes between two old stone gateposts and over two wooden footbridges before it ascends, (after a small wooden gate), out of the dip towards a tree, on a flagged path with a dry stone wall on your right.

> In the 1970s **Graining Water** used to be a popular unofficial camping spot because of the shelter it afforded and the running water. There were hardly any ferns there then but plenty abound now. It is, however, still a good place to stop for lunch or a break.

When you reach level ground again there is a guidepost with yellow directional arrows on it and an upside down white acorn on a black background (the symbol of a Long Distance Path – not the upside down bit though!). Continue ahead, with **Graining Water** on your left and a road (unseen) on your right. Just before **Well Hole Cottage** the path veers to the right via a short walled lane to the road. Here there is a PW signpost with **Hebble Hole** 3 mls pointing back and **Walshaw Res** 2 ml pointing left. Turn left along the tarmac road, passing **Well Hole Cottage** on your left. At the end of a lay-by on your right is another PW signpost with **High Gate Colden** 3 ml pointing back the way you have come, and **Walshaw Res** 1½ ml up the bank on your right. This takes you to the tarmac reservoir road where you turn right on it and follow it to a cattle grid. Just after the cattle grid, bear left on the road at a PW signpost with **Top Withins** 3 mls and **Widdop Rd** ½ ml.

Section 4.5

At a PW signpost, shortly before a track, which turns right, down to a reservoir dam (**Walshaw Dean Lower Reservoir**), turn right down the grass slope (wire fence on your right) to a stile in a wall ahead. Here you go half left to the track over the dam. Turn right on the track. Having crossed the dam, turn left onto a grassy track with the reservoir and a four-bar wooden fence on your left. At the end of the reservoir is another dam. Cross the gravel track and continue ahead past a PW signpost and a short wall on your left (do not turn left to cross the dam). At the end of the wall is a metal bridge over a concrete drainage ditch, which you cross. Continue ahead on an embankment with the reservoir (**Walshaw Dean Middle Reservoir**) on your left and a stone-bricked wide drainage ditch on your right. In the summer the path has loads of ferns and rhododendrons between you and the reservoir. Pass a narrow metal bridge on your right (do not cross) and shortly you will come to a second walled bridge with a PW signpost (**Widdop Road** 2 mls) where you cross (right) over the drainage ditch. Walk ahead to a gate in a wall. Shortly after the gate is a PW signpost directing you right, up an eroded path NE up the hillside. The path is slabbed in places. At the top of the slope, on a clear day, you may be lucky enough to see your last view of **Stoodley Pike** as you look back towards the reservoirs. A monocular, or a camera with a good zoom lens is useful here.

You descend towards **Top Withins** on a good flagged path. The flags meet a broken wall on the right and follows this round to **Top Withins** which is easily recognised by the two trees to the left of this ruined building.

Top Withins is quite a sad place. It was still occupied in the 1920s but by the 1950s it was abandoned and began to decay. A stone plaque on the side of the ruin (which incidentally refers to the building as Top Withens) dates to 1964 and refers to its association with Wuthering Heights in the Brontë novel of the same name. The building is a point of pilgrimage by Japanese as you will see further on where there are signs in Japanese on the PW signposts. My personal opinion is that the building should either have been carefully preserved in the 1960s when it still had much of its roof, or have been allowed to fall down and a suitable plaque placed there, marking the spot, instead of the rather sad concrete topped ruin that stands there today. The romance has been further decimated by the addition of a bothy (shelter) to the side of the ruin. On the positive side there are good views towards Haworth from the building, and it is a good sheltered place for a break.

Just past the ruin, the Brontë Way descends to the right. Here is one of the Japanese signposts. Continue ahead. You will find on this section of the PW a double set of flagstones. The only other double set is on the Border Ridge on the Scottish Borders. The first inhabited building you come to is called **Upper Heights**. This is an impressive new build on the site of an old farmhouse. The old farm used to provide camping and the new owners did apply for this again but to date it remains on a wish list. You next pass **Lower Heights**, then at the PW signpost turn left through a small wooden kissing gate, next to a metal gate, to descend down a walled lane to meet a track. Turn right on the track, then left on another track to **Buckley Farm**. Here you pass through a wooden gate and descend down a walled lane to **Rush Isles Farm**. At the tarmac road, you turn left onto it, round the edge of **Ponden Reservoir** passing **Ponden Hall** on the right. A bit further on the left is **Ponden Guest House**, which provides B&B. The lady of the house has a discreet campsite by Ponden Clough Beck if you wish to camp (there is a charge for camping, details are on the front door).

If you want to stay overnight at Haworth, where there are B&Bs, shops, banks etc and a Youth Hostel, after **Lower Heights** you need to continue ahead to reach a tarmac road, (Back Lane) which will take you into Stanbury. Here there is an infrequent bus service into Haworth or you can arrange for a taxi to pick you up from here. It can drop you back the following day at the same spot.

Section 5 – Ponden to Earby

Distance – 12.7 miles / 20.3 km
Height gained on PW route – 655 m (2,149 ft)
Height lost on PW route – 775 m (2,543 ft)

Route outline: Ponden Reservoir to Ickornshaw Moor; Nigher Dean Hole; Lumb; Ickornshaw; Middleton; Gill Bridge; Cowling Hill Lane; Woodhead Farm; Lothersdale; Pinhaw Beacon; Hare Hill; Gaylands Lane; Earby.

A good example of a stone step stile with sprung gate north of Lothersdale

Section 5.1

From **Ponden Guest House** continue ahead with the reservoir on your right. You will soon come to a wall and a PW signpost directing you ahead towards a farmhouse. This is the 'abandoned farmhouse' on page 130 of Wainwright's *Pennine Way Companion* (*Westmoreland*

Gazette edition). Continue ahead on a walled path with the farmhouse on your right, soon reaching another signpost where you bear right to a metal gate. Here you continue with the reservoir, now closer, on your right and you will shortly come to a bridge over the **River Worth** to a minor road.

Turn left along the road for a few yards until you come to a stone step stile in the wall on the opposite side of the road, next to a PW signpost. Cross the road and the stile and continue ahead, uphill, towards a gap in the wall to the NE. There should be a partially broken wall on your right as you ascend. After the gap in the wall, you cross a second wall via another stone step stile, and pass between two buildings (the one on the left is a ruin), to reach the house you could see from the road. Just before you reach the house you pass through a gate. Soon after you go through another gate. These are here to keep the owner's woolly pets from escaping. Ascend up the drive where, shortly on the left, you will see a wooden post on the bank on your left with 'Pennine Way' carved onto it vertically. Head towards it and continue in the same direction through two more gates and a kissing gate and a damp path along a wall, to meet another minor road (PW signpost).

Section 5.2

Turn left along the road, crossing a bridge over **Dean Clough**, and around a left hand bend in the road. After the second house on your left, on the opposite side of the road by a telegraph pole, is a PW signpost directing you up a wide track. After a bend in the track you meet a wall on your left (this wall will stay with you for the next mile). When the track bends to the right away from the wall, cross the wooden step stile in front of you, which is to the left of a metal gate next to the wall, and continue ahead passing through a gap, a stile and a second gap. When the wall ends (post on the right) continue ahead in the same direction to shortly reach **Old Bess Hill**. Here the obvious path swings NW passing to the right of a trig point on Little Wolf Stones in the distance, before swinging northwards once again. Intermittent slabs appear quite helpfully to guide you on your way. They are an improvement on what went before.

You are now on **Ickornshaw Moor**, which can be quite beautiful in sunny dry weather. The terrain appears quite flattish here. You will see the occasional wooden post or cairn but the slabs or the stony path underfoot makes the route reasonably easy to follow.

When you reach the crest of **Cat Stone Hill** you start descending towards **Nigher Dean Hole** and Cowling. Ahead you will soon see a stone cabin, with boards on the windows, and a wedged shaped side room on its left side. You will shortly bear right with a dry stone wall and pass several wooden creosoted cabins (called Cowlings) which shooters use in season. These are decades old but magnificently preserved by their owners. Time has stood still here. Keep an eye open for white painted letters PW with directional arrows on stones and the wall, or a 'PW' carved into a fence post. There are also a couple of helpful PW signposts here to guide you. Where the dry stone wall, which has been on your left the whole time, changes to a wire fence (with two ruins on the other side of it), keep a sharp eye open for a new galvanised metal gate (there used to be a ladder stile next to a gate here. The old gate was quite useful because when I walked the PW in 2011, the rungs on the south side of the stile were all missing). Go through the gate and descend on a grassy path between the two ruins with a wall on your left. You quickly descend down a steep bank, to some steps with a wooden handrail on your left, to reach a wooden footbridge, which you cross (**Nigher Dean Hole**). Ascend up the other side with a wire fence on your right. This will take you to a PW signpost. This is a good rest point on a sunny day (if you look back you should be able to see on a distant brown hill called Earl Crag, a pointy tower. This is Wainman's Pinnacle).

Section 5.3

From the signpost continue ahead to the track (wall on your left), and around a right hand bend. The small waterfall here is on **Lumb Head Beck**. Continue on the track, through a metal gate, and then when the track bends sharp left, continue ahead through a double gate which has a sheep pen on the left (there should be a newly built large barn on your right). After the gates, descend down a grassy walled lane to a small wooden gate in a wall. Ahead, across a track is **Lower Summer House Farm**. Go through the gate and cross the track. Pass through two more gates to reach a third gate in a fence with a PW signpost. Continue ahead across a field, under some power lines to reach the **A6068** road down some steps by a PW signpost. Cross the road. Ahead of you, you will see two PWs in white paint by a squeeze stile in the wall (which is now fenced off).

In the early days of the PW the squeeze stile took you down a slope and brought you down the side of a house where you passed in front of the kitchen and crossed into **Ickornshaw** village via a narrow stone bridge with iron railings on both sides. Wainwright on page 127 of his *Pennine Way Companion* called this *"an ingenious footway"*. Alas time has moved on and a probable change of ownership has brought about an amendment to the route.

Instead of crossing the squeeze stile, turn left along the pavement by the road until you shortly come to a PW signpost by a metal gate, which takes you down a slope to the village (**Ickornshaw**) where there is another PW signpost directing you to turn right.

You may have noticed a theme in the photographs used at the beginning of each section of the route description. The signage along the PW is as much a part of the PW as the scenery itself, and over the years these have changed in that they are more numerous with additional information provided. Note the change in PW signpost design here; this new design will continue for several miles.

Just before a building which looks a bit like a converted mill (a stone tablet in the building's wall says it was once a Wesleyan Chapel), a short lane comes in from the left (there should be a white PW painted on the telegraph pole with an arrow by the lane's entrance). Go up the lane to the end where there is a gate. Bear left then ahead with a wall on your right, go through a gate in a wall ahead, past some buildings, to a PW signpost at the end of the wall. Turn right along a track, past a garage, to the road (**Gill Lane**). Here are good views of Wainman's Pinnacle and Lund's Tower behind you on the right. Turn left down the lane, right at the T-junction, over **Gill Bridge** and then left (at the PW signpost) up a track past a bungalow. Here you follow a footpath, north, through a gate, then a stone step stile in a wall, then NW up the slope to a stile in a fence. Continue in the same direction to another stile (fence on the left of it and wall on the right) and ahead with a wall on your left up the slope to a large abandoned stone building in a poor state of repair. Go to the left of the building to cross a stile next to a PW signpost. Continue ahead up the slope on a faint grassy path through the field. Cross a stile in a wall (gate on the left) and ahead (wall on your right) to a second stile and PW signpost (**Gill Bottom** ¾ mls) onto a tarmac road (**Cowling Hill Lane**).

Section 5.4

Turn right on the minor road then left (PW signpost) on another minor road. The road descends to **Over House Farm** where it bends sharp left. When the road bends sharp right, continue ahead over a stone step stile. A PW signpost here says **Lothersdale** ¾ mls. Go down the grassy slope with a wall to your left, under some phone lines, through a gate in a stone wall, under power lines and across a muddy stream (**Surgill Beck**), which has a wooden gate (yellow directional arrow on the gate post) on the other side. The entrance to the beck is in some trees and is quite obscured so you may have to hunt for it. Go through the gate and continue in the same direction up the slope, with a line of trees on your right, to another gate, which is the entrance to **Woodhead Farm**.

Woodhead Farm used to be quite famous in the early days of the PW. Ethel Burnup, who died in July 1990 at the age of 80, was in the very first Pennine Way Association accommodation guide and at one time she had an incredible 16 beds for what she called her "Pennine Highwaymen". Her hospitality and care of walkers was second to none, as were her enormous breakfasts. Tom Stephenson often stopped by her place to see her whenever he was in the area. She was one of the originals. In her twilight years she continued to provide B&B but in a more haphazard way. I once got rice and potatoes on the same plate and a flower vase instead of a glass, but we all loved her. She was fantastic but alas she has now gone. The farm has been sold and it has been developed into multiple residential dwellings with beautifully maintained gardens.

Pass through the 'farm' up a tarmac road with the buildings on your right and the gardens on the left. Shortly after the cattle grid, turn right off the road by a PW signpost, and descend down the slope with a broken wall on your right.

From here there are good views of the village, the old textile mill chimney and the wooded valley along the line of Stansfield Beck. This cuts off the road corner and takes you into **Lothersdale**. The PW leaves the village to the left of the large barn that you can see to the west of the trees.

At the bottom of the slope, turn right onto the road, across the road bridge over **Lothersdale Beck** and, just after the Hare and Hounds pub, turn left at the PW sign (**White Hill Lane** ¾ ml) up a gravel track to a gate in a wall, by a large pile of stones (the large barn is at the end of the track). Immediately past the gate there is a PW signpost directing you left up the slope (wooden then wire fence, then wall on your left). You follow the fence / wall northwards to a wooden step stile with a small sprung gate above it. Cross and continue ahead to a PW signpost next to a stone step stile in the wall to your right. Again there is a small sprung wooden gate on top (see photograph at beginning of this section). Cross the stile and continue NW, with a wall on your right, to reach a wooden gate and the road. Cross the road and continue ahead up a tarmac lane to **Hewitts Farm**. Where the road bends left to the farm, continue ahead, through a gate, into a partially walled lane, to a stone step stile (sprung gate on top) in another wall, which crosses your path. After the wall the path is slabbed. The wall and PW curve to the left after a manhole cover on the right of the path. When the wall turns sharply to the left, continue ahead on the obvious path to **Pinhaw Beacon**. There is a trig point on the top (S 4451) and fine views on sunny days.

Section 5.5

Leave the trig point, on the same obvious path descending SW to a wall with a PW signpost. Along this section of the route there may be a daunting sign saying 'Beware Adders'. At the wall the path turns right (wall on your left) and takes you to a tarmac road where the PW signpost informs you that **Thornton-in-Craven** is 1½ miles distant.

There is no accommodation for walkers in **Thornton-in-Craven**. Even the railway station, which was on the Leeds and Bradford Extension Railway from Colne to Skipton, (opened on 2 October 1848, and was still there when the PW was opened in 1965), has gone. The line closed to passengers in 1970 and the rails were later removed.

Cross the road and continue ahead on a tarmac road (**Clogger Lane**) with open countryside on your right and a wall on your left.

This is **Elslack Moor** where Tom Stephenson famously posed, hand against a wooden sign, which said 'No Road. Any person found trespassing upon this Moor or taking dogs thereon will be prosecuted'. There is a painting based on this photograph in the common room at the youth hostel in **Dufton**.

About 300 yards down the road look out for a ladder stile slightly away from the road on your left, next to a wooden gate. On the stone gatepost is painted 'YHA' with a directional arrow. You can reach Earby youth hostel from here (see directions in the box below) or you can continue on the PW and cut off for the hostel further along the PW.

Leave the road and climb the stile or go through the gate. The descending grassy path (restricted byway) will take you to Earby youth hostel where you will receive a warm welcome. There are shops and a pub there too. The grassy lane leads to Hawber Lane and Gaylands Lane heading SW and there is a path (signed) to the youth hostel over a stream. If you miss that turnoff you continue to the end of the lane where you turn left up the road and the hostel is in the village.

Continue on the Pennine Way for an alternative route to Earby YH. At the ladder stile on **Elslack Moor**, cross the ladder stile and continue NW down the slope with the wall on your right, over a section of wooden duckboards to cross a stone step stile (sprung gate on top) in a wall crossing the path. Continue down the slope, crossing a second section of duckboards. You will soon come to a PW signpost, where you cross a narrow wooden footbridge. A second PW signpost at the other end of the footbridge directs you to bear left, down the slope to a metal gate in a stone wall, with a small squeeze stile on the left. Bear slightly left and descend across the field to a wooden kissing gate (Wood House Farm is on the hill above to your right) in a gap in the line of trees ahead. Here descend to a kissing gate where you cross a stream to a final gate (the ground is quite churned up by the hooves of cattle), reaching the farm road just before **Brown House Farm**.

To reach Earby youth hostel from here, you walk ahead between the two large farm buildings to a gate. Go through this and follow the faint path above Earby Beck (on the right) to Booth Bridge. Here you follow a path half left up the slope to Batty House where a track will take you down to the tarmac road in the village. Turn left here and walk up the road to the youth hostel. Retrace your steps back to the Brown House Farm in the morning. This alternative route saves you a bit of time and distance. It would be useful to have the relevant section of the 1:25 000 map here to help you with your walk into Earby. There are stiles and the paths are obvious but there are no helpful PW signposts to guide you here as you are off route (the *Pennine Way South AZ Adventure Atlas* covers Earby).

Section 6 – Earby to Malham

Distance – 12.4 miles / 20 km
Height gained on PW route – 305 m (1,001 ft)
Height lost on PW route – 160 m (525 ft)

Route outline: Earby to Thornton-in-Craven; Leeds-Liverpool Canal; Scaleber Hill; Gargrave; Eshton Moor; Newfield Bridge; Airton; Hanlith; Malham.

On route between Gargrave and Eshton Moor

If you stayed at the youth hostel, and took the route via Gaylands Lane, and you don't want to walk all the way back to the PW on Elslack Moor, you can take the lane to Batty House Farm and the footpath to Booth Bridge. From here there is a footpath on the east bank of Brown House Beck, which takes you to the right (East) of Brown House Farmhouse (to a gate between two large farm buildings) where you can rejoin the PW.

For the purists, who arrived at the hostel via Gaylands Lane, make your way back to the ladder stile on Elslack Moor (but don't cross it). Turn left at the ladder stile and continue NW down the slope with the wall on your right, over a section of wooden duckboards to cross a stone step stile (sprung gate on top) in a wall crossing the path. Continue down the slope, crossing a second section of duckboards. You will soon come to a PW signpost, where you cross a narrow wooden footbridge. A second PW signpost at the other end of the footbridge directs you to bear left, down the slope to a metal gate in a stone wall, with a small squeeze stile on the left. Bear slightly left and descend across the field to a wooden kissing gate (Wood House Farm is on the hill above to your right) in a gap in the line of trees ahead. Here descend to a kissing gate where you cross a stream to a final gate (the ground is quite churned up by the hooves of cattle), reaching the farm road just before **Brown House Farm**.

Section 6.1

Having descended the slope from Wood House, when you reach the tarmac lane, bear half right (westwards) along the lane, past **Brown House Farm**, over a cattle grid, over a bridge over **Brown House Beck**, over a second cattle grid and across the line of the old railway, (although you won't see it as you are on a tarmac road, however the old railway bridge abutments are still there on both sides of the road), to a T-junction (PW signpost), where you turn left and go under a stone bridge. Continue down this road to **Thornton-in-Craven**.

At a PW signpost, go (right) up a grassy bank to the **A56**. Opposite you is **Cam Lane**, which you go up, passing several bungalows on either side, until you come to a cattle grid by a shed. Shortly afterwards, with a house on your left and a large barn on your right, look out for a yellow PW sign on a wooden gatepost (at the end of the barn) on the right-hand side of the lane, next to a signpost. The sign says 'Private Road to Langber Farm only. Pennine Way across the field' (half right). This path takes you to a gate in a fence with a hedgerow in it. Go through the gate and descend (slightly west of north) to a slab bridge over a stream. Ascend out of the dip, through two gates in fences passing a marker stone on the crest of the hill (**Town Hill**). Continuing in roughly the same direction, cross a wooden step stile in a fence, go under some power lines and descend to a galvanised metal gate in a fence, over a plank bridge (rail on the left side), cross a boggy area and ascend up the bank ahead to another metal gate to meet the towpath of the **Leeds-Liverpool Canal**.

Section 6.2

Turn right with the canal on your left. This is nice and flat, as you would expect. You will soon come to a stone bridge over the canal (**Bridge 160**). Do not cross it but continue ahead. You next come to a double arched bridge (**Bridge 161**), which serves the dual function of a canal bridge, and the higher **A59** road bridge. Go under the bridge. As you ascend the bank of the next bridge (**Bridge 162**) you will see a PW signpost by the bridge. The longer finger post pointing back the way you have come tells you that you have travelled 1½ miles since **Thornton-in-Craven**. This bridge will take you into East Marton if you are seeking refreshments. The next PW signpost seems to inform you that **Bridge 162** is called **Trenet Bridge** whereas the OS map calls it **Williamson Bridge**. Continue ahead on a lane, which runs parallel with the canal.

After about a quarter of a mile, leave the lane at a PW signpost by a gate. There is also a yellow PW directional marker on the gatepost. Here you go NE, cutting off the corner of the lane. You could keep on the lane but that wouldn't be the Pennine Way would it? You pass a wooden fence on your left, go through a small swing gate in a wooden fence and enter a small wooded area (wall on your right). A few yards into the wooded area you cross a large stone step stile with a wooden fence across it. Not long after, you leave the wooded area by another small wooden swing gate in a wooden fence and rejoin the track at another wooden step stile. The PW signpost tells you that you have travelled ½ mile since East Marton.

Go right, along the track, crossing **Crickle Beck** by a bridge on the track. Shortly afterwards, at a T-junction, bear left, (**Trenet Laithe** is the house on the right) then leave the lane by crossing a stone step stile on the right (this section between the canal and **Gargrave** is over low rolling hills and requires some concentration to avoid getting lost as the path can be quite faint in places despite the PW being almost 50 years old). Walk ahead to a large wooden footbridge (the old plank footbridge and stile are beside it on the right, although they may have been removed), cross this and go through a metal gate. Continue ahead, crossing two stiles in two fences, which cross your path. There are plenty of yellow directional arrows here to aid navigation, so keep an eye open for them. Soon after you cross a track. Keep ahead, in the same direction, to a metal gate in a fence, to a second (kissing) gate, crossing over **Crickle Beck** (for a second time), and on to a stile in a fence. Ahead once again, up the slope to a stone trough on the right, then over two stiles in wire fences to a gate in a fence. Keep ahead to meet a track by a four (short) finger signpost with 'FP' on two of them, and 'Pennine Way' on the other two. Ahead in the distance is **Gargrave** Church. Go ahead on the track, over a stile next to a metal gate, to meet a larger track to Scaleber Farm by a cattle grid, with a wooden bench on your right. This is a quiet spot if you need a rest or need time to gather your thoughts before you go into **Gargrave**, the next stop.

Section 6.3
Go initially NNE on the Scaleber Farm road, through a gate, then over a railway bridge (**Mosber Lane Bridge**). Just past the bridge, look out for a signpost on the right and some steps up to a small metal gate

which directs you across a field, through two metal gates in fences (one fence is wooden and the other half wire and half wooden) that cross your route, and onto a section of flagged path with a tall wall on your left. The building here used to be a school but it is now a private house with the creative name 'Pennine Way'! Cross the stile in the wall after you pass the building and turn right, away from the house to meet a T-junction where you turn left, passing the very picturesque church.

Set into the wall here, by the road, is a blue plaque dedicated to the Rt Hon Iain Macleod (1913–1970) MP for Enfield West, who held several ministerial positions before becoming Chancellor of the Exchequer. 'A post he held for only three weeks before his untimely death'.

Continue past the church over a bridge over the **River Aire** to meet the **A65** at the crossroads.

In front of you is the famous Dalesman Café Tearooms and Sweet Emporium, which has a PW book, which walkers can sign. On your right are the public toilets. Note the interesting metal PW signpost to the left of the café (see photograph at the end of the *History of the Pennine Way* section). This tells you that you have walked 70 miles so far and that you have 186 miles still to go! There is a nice area by the stream with benches where you can have a quiet lunch if you wish. There is also a railway station in **Gargrave**, which is quite handy if you need to break your journey here.

Section 6.4

The PW takes the road ahead of you, (**West Street**), passing the Dalesman Café on your left in the process.

First though, please note that **Gargrave** is one of the major shopping villages on the route and you should therefore use it wisely. The next town with good shops is **Hawes**, several days distant. In **Gargrave** there are pubs, an ATM machine and a Co-op food store and other shops. They are all along the A65 to your right.

When you have finished any business that you have with **Gargrave**, return to the bridge and go up **West Street**. You will shortly pass over the **Leeds-Liverpool Canal** where a metal signpost tells you that **Malham** is 5¾ miles away (there is a canal lock on your left and it is worth spending a few minutes here if a canal boat is about to use it). Continue up the lane, past the extensive grounds of **Gargrave House** on the left. Further up the lane, on the left, is a house called **New Barn**, which used to be an old barn but has recently been redeveloped into a fine looking, rather large house. There are benches along this lane (**Mark House Lane**), which the local dog walkers probably use. As you climb the slope up the lane, keep an eye open for a PW sign on your right, under the shelter of the trees. It informs you that **Airton** is 3 miles away. Climb up the bank by the signpost to cross a stone step stile in the wall.

From the stone step stile, head uphill, half left, to a wooden stile on the right of a wooden gate. Cross the stile, walk to the fence corner a few yards ahead, then walk up the slope to another gate with a kissing gate next to it. Continue up the slope to a prominent signpost, by the corner of a fenced wood (**Middle Plantation**). Here you bear half left to a kissing gate in a wire fence, and continue in roughly the same direction to a second kissing gate in a fence. Continue ahead towards the corner of a second wood and signpost (**Harrows Hill**). Turn left at the wall, and walk to the wall corner where there is a gate and PW signpost. Go through the gate and head NNW to another wall, entering a walled lane where there are two gates close together.

Go through the gates and head half left (NW) across a grass field, with the wall initially on your left, towards a three-fingered PW signpost. The third finger points to the left to Bell Busk.

You are quite likely to encounter one or more bulls during your PW walk. There may be a bull in this field so keep your eyes open! They are reasonably short sighted but do give them a wide berth if you come across one, and walk at a measured, but not too brisk pace. If there are plenty of cows in the same field, he will hopefully be distracted by them, but do keep your eyes on them until you are out of his reach.

After the signpost, continue in the same direction, down the slope of **Eshton Moor**, until you come to a narrowing with a wall on your left, and the road to **Malham** on your right. Between the two is a wooden fence with a small wooden gate in it. Go through the gate. Follow the wall round to the left, passing through a gate to cross a wooden footbridge over the **River Aire**.

Section 6.5

Continue in the direction of the bridge, with the river on your right, passing through two gates and a stile to reach the road at **Newfield Bridge**. Just before the bridge you have to cross a wooden step stile in a wooden fence on your left, before ascending some stone steps to a squeeze stile, which takes you to the road. The PW signpost here tells you that you have walked 3 miles from **Gargrave**. Turn right on the road, to the other end of the bridge, and at the PW signpost on the left (**Airton** ¾ ml), descend the squeeze stile in the wall, and go down the bank to the riverside with the **River Aire** now on your left. Continue along the riverside, crossing several stone stepped stiles to climb up more stone steps (wooden grab rail on the left) to reach **Airton Bridge**. The PW signpost tells you that you are now 4 miles from **Gargrave**. Cross the road and descend to the riverside again. The PW signpost on the opposite side of the road informs you that

Hanlith is 1⅓ miles ahead. After a short distance you will come to a small wooden gate in a wall with a wooden footbridge behind it. Go through the gate and cross the bridge. There is another PW signpost here, telling you that you have travelled ⅓ mile and that **Airton** is also ⅓ mile away to the west. Your next point of note is a brick pump house in between two fences, which you cross by means of kissing gates. Next you cross a sike via another footbridge. Here you continue ahead while the **River Aire** curves away to your left. When it comes back to meet you, you pass through a very small plantation by means of two wooden gates, only yards apart, with a wooden fence on your left and the trees on your right. Go through one more kissing gate in a fence and the next point of reference is **Hanlith Bridge**. Here you have travelled 1⅓ miles since **Airton** according to the PW signpost.

Section 6.6

Turn right up the road, up a steep incline, past **Hanlith Hall** on your right, to a fork in the road. Take the left fork and continue up the hill. When the road bends very sharply to the right, look out for a PW signpost (**Malham** 1 mile) on the left by a gate in a wall. The signpost is by a tree so it may be obscured by foliage. Go up the steps to the gate and pass through. You are now on a faint grassy walk, high above the **River Aire** (on your left). **Malham Cove** will shortly come into view ahead. You will pass through numerous gates in walls on the way to **Malham**, as this is a prime tourist honey pot. Between a small stone slab footbridge (**Black Hole Bridge**) and a Barn (**Mires Barn**) is Aire Head, the source of the River Aire.

> The water that emerges from the base of **Malham Cove** is **Malham Beck**, not the source of the **River Aire**. This has been proven by dyes placed in the stream, which emerges from **Malham Tarn**, further north.

About ¼ mile beyond the barn you will reach the southern tip of **Malham**. There is an old clapper bridge raised on plinths here, next to a stone building with a 'No Fishing' sign on its walls. Cross the beck here and turn right up the road to enter **Malham** village proper. The **Buck Inn**, one of two pubs in the village is here. Where the road branches off to the right, by a whitewashed building with ice cream signs outside (the Post Office), turn off right and cross over the road bridge. On the left, in front of a small village green, is the Lister Arms Hotel. Ahead is the youth hostel. If you want to camp, don't take the right fork but go straight ahead after you pass the **Buck Inn**, up **Cove Road**. **Town Head Farm** campsite is just before the turn off for **Malham Cove**. There are plenty of B&Bs in the village.

Section 7 – Malham to Horton-in-Ribblesdale

Distance – 14.2 miles / 22.9 km
Height gained on PW route – 800 m (2,625 ft)
Height lost on PW route – 770 m (2,526 ft)

Route outline: Malham to Malham Cove; Watlowes; Malham Tarn; Tennant Gill Farm; Fountains Fell; Rainscar House; Dale Head Farm; Pen-y-ghent; Horton Scar Lane; Horton-in-Ribblesdale.

Pen-y-ghent from road below Fountains Fell

Section 7.1

Return to **Cove Road** and head northwards along it. After passing **Town Head Farm** campsite entrance on your right, look out for a small wooden gate (with 'Peregrine viewpoint this way' on it), and a PW signpost on the other side of the wall (**Malham Cove** ½ ml; **Malham Tarn** 1¾ ml), also on your right. Go through the gate down a white gravelled path towards **Malham Cove**. Go through a wooden gate in a wall ahead, and continue to a second wall with a gate in it. After the gate bear left up some steps, through a gate, continuing up the steps which take you up the left side of **Malham Cove** until you meet a wall and a PW signpost. Here care is needed, to avoid being misplaced, and to avoid twisting your ankle (or worse) on the limestone pavement on the top of **Malham Cove**. You need to head eastwards, parallel with the cove edge (but away from it), until you meet a wall with a signpost and a ladder stile. Don't cross the stile but turn left with the wall and head NNW with the wall now on your right. You are now entering a dry valley called **Watlowes**. A reasonably defined track appears and you then cross a wall ahead via either of the two stiles with spring gates on top. Continuing northwards you cross a wooden step stile in a wooden fence which crosses the path, then shortly, you reach the valley end and start ascending, what is now a shallow dry waterfall, with a wall on your right. At the top you will find a stile (which you cross) and a PW signpost, which informs you that you have travelled ½ mile from **Malham Cove** and **Malham Tarn** is 1 mile ahead.

Here you turn right on a good track with a wire fence on your right, and good views back down the valley you have just walked up. The path takes you up another short valley with crags on both sides and a cave on the crag on the left. When you exit this valley you continue ahead, then the path bears left towards a PW signpost with **Malham Cove** 1½ miles pointing back towards where you have walked from. Ahead you should be able to see the Tarn and a car park.

This area, around Malham Lings, was used for the official opening of the Pennine Way on 24 April 1965, and again in 1985 to celebrate the 50th anniversary of the famous newspaper article by Tom Stephenson, *'Wanted – A Long Green Trail'* which appeared in the *Daily Herald* on 22 June 1935 (see *History of the Pennine Way* for information on this article).

Section 7.2

Walk towards the car park, and you will come to a tarmac road, a kissing gate, and a PW signpost (**Malham Cove** is still 1½ miles behind you). At the entrance to the car park opposite is another PW signpost (**Malham Tarn** ¼ mile; **Waterhouses** 1¾ miles). Proceed ahead, with the car park on your right, passing the southern tip of **Malham Tarn** (**Tarn Foot**) on your left. The path swings to the right, skirting a walled plantation called **Lings Plantation**, (occasionally there is a bull there), and then ahead to join a track, where you turn left and you should continue along it to **Malham Tarn House**.

> **Malham Tarn House** was originally built as a shooting lodge by Lord Lister in the 1780s, but was extensively rebuilt by Walter Morrison, and it is now owned by the National Trust who lease it to the Field Studies Council.

Walk past the house and at a fork in the track, go left on the main track which descends through the woods.

Just before a building on the right (**Water Houses**), look out for a wooden gate on the right and a PW signpost, which says 'Tennant Gill 1½ miles'. Go through the gate onto an obvious grassy path round the boundary wall then ahead to a second wooden gate, (with a stone step stile and small sprung gate on top, next to it) which you pass through. Continue on the grassy path with a wall on your left, to pass a stone barn on the left. Walk ahead with the wall still on your left, round a walled enclosure, with another barn in it (Great Hill), and go through a kissing gate in the wall ahead. There is a tree to the left of the kissing gate. (There used to be an awkward ladder stile here, and I am pleased to say these are being phased out and replaced with easier small gates and kissing gates.) Ahead in the distance is **Tennant Gill Farm** in the trees. You now gradually descend to the wall corner where a PW signpost directs you left, with the wall, down the slope. You head towards the road via a stile in the wall ahead. After crossing this you walk NNW to another PW signpost at the road. This one tells you that **Waterhouses** (their spelling not mine) is 1⅓ miles behind and **Dalehead** is 5½ miles ahead. This particular signpost is very imaginatively set into the top of the wall using a metal fencepost spike,

Section 7.3

Bear right, on the road, cross the cattle grid and go up the track to **Tennant Gill Farm**, passing a huge barn on your right, then ahead, uphill to a stone wall with a wooden gate, stone step stile and a PW signpost. Cross the stile and go left, following the wall on your left to another PW signpost, which directs you right (NW), along the line of an old wall (which will be on your left as you walk). After about 500 yards you come to another PW signpost, which directs you right (NNE), away from the wall. You are now following an old miners' track, northwards initially, then northwest up the flanks of **Fountains Fell**. It is easy to follow in good weather. Large sections of it have been gravelled. Initially you cross **Tennant Gill**, and ascend to a small wooden gate in a wall, (there is a larger wooden field gate a few yards to the right of it). As you ascend, don't forget to look back here as there is a good view of **Malham Tarn** from just beyond the gate. Continue your gradual ascent. Later you descend down some stone steps to cross a stream. You then head NW to eventually reach a sign which says 'There are a number of open shafts in this area. Please keep to the footpath'. The path near the summit of **Fountains Fell** is quite rocky and uncomfortable to walk on. Hopefully it will be upgraded sometime. Soon after the sign, you will pass two tall cairns on your right. Here **Pen-y-ghent** and Ingleborough come into view ahead. Shortly after the two cairns you come to a wall running down the flank of **Fountains Fell**. There is a stone step stile here, which allows you to cross it.

You are now at the highest point of your walk over **Fountains Fell** and it is a good place to stop for a break, as the wall makes a good windbreak. The actual summit of **Fountains Fell** is about ¼ mile away to your left (SW).

On the opposite side of the wall is a tall post with an acorn carved into it and a yellow directional arrow. Cross the wall and continue ahead on the track, (another old mine track) which soon veers to the left, giving great views of **Pen-y-ghent**. The descent is along a grassy, springy path with a good steady descent. When you meet a wall ahead, turn right with the wall, now on your far left, and continue to descend to a kissing gate (slabs either side) in a crossing wall, then onto a tarmac road at a cattle grid. The PW signpost here says '**Malham Tarn** 6 ml' (see photograph at the beginning of this section).

Section 7.4

Turn left on the tarmac road, passing **Rainscar House Farm** on your right and, shortly afterwards, a barn on your left (the dry stone walls around here have huge quantities of moss on them). Shortly after a gate in the road, you turn right up a farm road to **Dale Head Farm**. The PW signpost here tells you that the PW is now on a Byway Open to All Traffic and 'Helwith Bridge is 2¾ ml' (did you notice how the profile of **Pen-y-ghent** changed as you walked along the road and farm track?). Just past the farm you go through a gate across the track. Continue on the track through a second gate to a PW signpost (**Pen-y-ghent** 1 mile to the right and Helwith Bridge to the left), which directs you right up another track, which leads to a path and later to some wooden duckboards. Follow these towards the now stern-like profile of **Pen-y-ghent**.

The duckboards swing to the left after a while, towards a wall corner, and you should cross the dry stone wall ahead via a stone step stile. The path continues to ascend towards **Pen-y-ghent** on a narrow path, with the wall on your left. Your next landmark is a PW signpost with an additional pointer to the left indicating that Bracken Bottom is 1¼ miles down a rocky (at times) and sometimes steep path. The PW continues ahead.

> If you don't want to climb **Pen-y-ghent** you can get to **Horton-in-Ribblesdale** by taking the Brackenbottom path (the OS maps has Brackenbottom as one word rather than the two on the signpost). There is a good view of the quarry at Horton slightly before you reach the signpost. It is strange to see a quarry in a National Park but the former existed before the latter.

At the signpost the ascent increases. The path underfoot is now stoned and later there are steps up the steeper slopes.

> Now is the time to get out your walking pole. That 'third leg' will help you balance as you lean into the slope. The path up **Pen-y-ghent** looks awful due to the fact that it isn't just part of the Pennine Way but it is more frequently used by day walkers and people walking the Three Peaks (Whernside and Ingleborough are the other two peaks) where the idea is to walk a circular route, starting from the **Pen-y-ghent Café** in **Horton-in-Ribblesdale** (you must register before starting off and the café is closed on Tuesdays so you can't record your finish and get your certificate on a Tuesday) taking in all three peaks in the same day.

Seen from the side (especially from **Fountains Fell**), **Pen-y-ghent** resembles a crouching lion. The 'nose' of the lion forms the first section of the ascent after the signpost and the PW curves to the right to ascend this to avoid a rock climb. Once you reach the 'nose' it levels off for a short distance and here you leave the limestone behind temporarily (at the 600 metres / 2,000 feet contour) and meet gritstone; the wall on your left changes colour to reflect this. You now have a second steep climb before the path levels off and there is a gradual ascent to the summit of **Pen-y-ghent** where you will find a trig point (S 5776) built of stone and a small cairn.

What is most unusual here is that there are two stiles, side by side in the summit wall by the trig point. This shows just how popular this hill can be in the summer. There are good views across the valley to **Fountains Fell** from the wall. The wall provides some shelter from the wind (**Pen-y-ghent** means 'hill of the winds') so in good weather it is a nice place to stop for a break. I usually carry a half litre lightweight flask of coffee for just such an occasion. The wall here is curved and there are seats here too!

By the wall is a PW signpost directing you to **Horton-in-Ribblesdale**. **Dale Head** is behind you, and the third finger of the signpost points right, to Plover Hill, which is 1⅓ miles away. The descent is quite obvious. It is the white-looking man-made strip of a path, initially descending NW, then NNE, then westwards, then SW. Before you reach the limestone crags the path does a 90 degree turn to the left and continues on its descent to reach a wall with a stone step stile and a gate in it. Go through the gate (or cross the stile) and continue ahead. A wall comes in from the left and you meet a second wall ahead, with two ladder stiles and a gate, which you cross. Walk ahead on the path to the entrance of **Horton Scar Lane**. (To your right is Hull Pot, which is worth a detour. If you go to Hull Pot, retrace your steps back to the wall and the PW signpost there, which has a Trailblaze box on it.) You are now 1¾ miles from **Pen-y-ghent** and 1½ miles from **Horton-in-Ribblesdale**. Turn left, through a gate, to enter **Horton Scar Lane**. (Tomorrow you will leave **Horton-in-Ribblesdale** via **Harber Scar Lane**.) Follow the lane, through a gate, past the ruined stone barn on the left, and through a second gate. Turn right through a third gate at a fork in the lane and walk down to the tarmac road. Here the PW signpost tells you that **Pen-y-ghent** is 3¼ miles away. The smaller finger post directs you to turn right.

The Golden Lion Inn (which has a bunkhouse), Holme Farm campsite and the church are down the road to your left. A few yards along the road to the right is a white building, the infamous **Pen-y-ghent Café** which has been run by the Bayes family for two generations (Peter then Matthew). It has the first and most famous Pennine Way Logbook. If you have walked the PW before and signed one of the dozens of volumes of the logbook, they will still have it. I don't know which came first, the PW or the café but they are almost synonymous when you think of the walk. They do pint mugs of tea and coffee, cooked meals, as well as selling books and maps, chocolate bars and other snacks, walking gear, fuel; the list is endless. The café is also the Tourist Information Centre so they can recommend accommodation for you. Try and book your accommodation in Horton early in your route planning, if you can as it is a small village with a limited number of beds. Although there are two hotels, and some B&Bs plus a campsite and bunkhouse, it gets busy during the summer months.

Section 8 – Horton-in-Ribblesdale to Hawes

Distance – 13.7 miles / 22 km
Height gained on PW route – 510 m (1,673 ft)
Height lost on PW route – 460 m (1,509 ft)

Route outline: Horton-in-Ribblesdale to Sell Gill Holes; Jackdaw Hole; Old Ing; Cam End; Kidhow Gate; West Cam Road; Ten End; Gaudy Lane; Gayle; Hawes.

Half-way point between Horton-in-Ribblesdale and Hawes

Section 8.1

Having left **Horton Scar Lane** and turned right up the main road through the village, past the **Pen-y-ghent Café** on the left, you leave **Horton-in-Ribblesdale** by walking up the tarmac in front of entrance to **The Crown Inn** (shown as the **New Inn** on some OS maps) and in the left corner of the forecourt is a PW signpost pointing left, to

Birkwith Moor, which is 3 miles away. It also says that the PW here is a restricted byway (what it doesn't tell you is that you also share the footpath with the Ribble Way for a short distance). You enter a walled lane, not unlike the one you walked down yesterday, except this one is uphill. (As you climb out of the village, look back at the views of the quarry, and across at **Pen-y-ghent**. Both are worth a photograph if the light is good.) The walled lane is called **Harber Scar Lane** and at its end is a gate with a stile beside it. Cross this. There is now only one proper wall, which is on your left. On your right, the wall gradually disappears to show open fell. At the next gate, on the right, before the path becomes a walled lane again, is **Sell Gill Holes**. Shortly after, the Ribble Way leaves the PW. Go through the gate, soon passing a signpost with 'Birkwith 1⅞ miles' on it, then a ruined barn on your left. Continue ahead, with the wall on your left. The next landmarks to look out for, after a gate, are a few trees on the left, in a fenced area, on the opposite side of the wall. This is **Jackdaw Hole**.

Still heading north on the obvious track, go through another gate, later passing a stone step stile on the left (ignore this – it goes to Birkwith Cave). Further on you cross a small stream and pass through a gate in the wall ahead. The large plantation on Old Ing Moor directly ahead should be getting closer. You ascend up the incline to cross another stream in a dip, larger than the first one, and go through a gate in the wall ahead. Here you will find a three-finger signpost. The one pointing back tells you that you have travelled 3 miles since leaving **Horton-in-Ribblesdale**. Ahead is High Green Field. Up the bank on your left ½ mile distant, is **Old Ing** farm, your next objective. Climb the bank to a gate, next to a stone step stile, and descend along the path to meet a farm track and PW signpost.

Section 8.2

Turn left on the track. In the trees ahead on the left is **Old Ing**. Before that is a barn with a strangely shaped roof. Pass the barn and the farm, after which the track turns sharp right. There is another signpost here informing you that our old friend the Pennine Bridleway joins us once more. You turn right with the track (a restricted byway) towards **Cam End**, through a gate. The next gate has the picturesque **Calf Holes** (**Dry Lathe** on OS map) on the right, where the stream disappears underground. The track slopes slightly uphill towards some trees and you pass a barn, over the wall on the left. You then start descending towards **Ling Gill Beck**, which is crossed by **Ling Gill Bridge**.

This is a great place to stop for a boots off break. A stone plaque in the wall of the bridge draws attention to what was once a very important bridge on an ancient packhorse road. It says that in 'Anno 1765, this bridge was repaired at the charge of the whole West Rideing'. Wainwright said that the bridge dates back to the 16th Century. Frank Duerden also said that the bridge was built two hundred years earlier at the expense of John Sigeswicke of Cam, who left forty shillings in his will to pay for it.

Suitably refreshed, continue up the track where, at **Cam End**, the PW and the Pennine Bridleway join the Dales Way for a mile or so, and the Pennine Bridleway for a longer distance. There is a signpost here.

There are good views of the Ribblehead Viaduct and its 24 arches which tower 105 feet above Batty Moss in the distance on your left. The viaduct is on the famous Settle to Carlisle Railway, one of England's most scenic railways. It opened to passenger traffic in 1876 and has 72 miles of track, 20 major viaducts and 14 tunnels. It is a wonderful piece of engineering and was once threatened with closure as part of a cost saving exercise, but the public outcry and the strategic importance of the line won out in the end. It is now very popular with walkers, especially in the summer months or when steam trains run along it.

Turn to the right, onto **Cam High Road**. The OS maps say that this is an old Roman Road. The first gate in a crossing wall that you pass through is **West Gate**. Soon after, just before the Dales Way descends into the valley on the right, there is a cairn and a signpost.

> The cairn and signpost can be seen above in the photograph at the beginning of this section. This new cairn is better built that its predecessor. The old signpost (replaced sometime between July 2011 and 2012) used to say that you are exactly halfway between **Horton-in-Ribblesdale** and **Hawes** (6½ miles each way), but you will find no mileage on the current one.

Continue ahead on the PW and the Pennine Bridleway, through a second gate. Soon after the track surface changes from being sandy to tarmac. A turn off to the right is the access road to Cam Farm. The next gate in the road is called **Cold Keld Gate**. Here there is a three-fingered signpost (one for the Pennine Way ahead to **Ten End**, 4 miles distant; a second pointing back the way you have come showing the Pennine Way and the Pennine Bridleway; and a third for the Pennine Bridleway where it turns off to the Newby Head Road).

Section 8.3

Go through the gate and continue ahead to another (less elaborate) PW signpost where you leave the tarmac (just before Kidhow Gate) and turn left along a wide grassy track called **West Cam Road**. Dodd Fell is on your right and Snaizeholme Valley is on your left. You soon come to a wall on your left and a slope on your right. You go through a gate, and the wall on your left is replaced by a wire fence for a short section, before reverting back to a wall again. There is a small section of walled lane after another gate and then you are in open country. At a PW signpost, **(Ten End Peat Ground)** where the track starts to descend to the left, go slightly right (NE) up a grassy path. **Gaudy Lane** is 2 miles away according to the signpost here.

The path is quite clear at this point, with cairns to help navigation. You ascend a slight incline to a wall, and then descend to a gate, which you go through. Continue in the same direction on a grassy path, to see a prominent cairn on the hill to your left. The path descends to a stream, which you cross and you need to go through a wooden gate in the wall ahead. You now descend with a wall on your right, passing through two wooden gates, a gap in the wall, and a third gate, then down through rough pasture (wall now on your left) to meet a metal gate and a tarmac road by **Gaudy House Farm**.

On the descent, **Hawes** is clearly visible ahead. If you look to your left you should just about make out the settlement of **Hardraw**. There is a rounded ridge, which gently rises on the left, and then curves around to the right. This is the beginning of your route tomorrow, as the PW climbs **Bluebell Hill**, then **Little Fell, Black Hill Moss, Crag End, Hearne Head** and finally you reach the summit of **Great Shunner Fell**.

Section 8.4

The PW signpost by the tarmac road tells you that **Ten End** is 2 miles behind you. Cross the stile between the wall and the gate and turn right down the road. When you come to a T-junction (stone barn on the right), turn right on another tarmac road, then a few yards later, at a PW signpost (**West End** ¼ ml), go through a small wooden sprung gate in the wall on your left and continue ahead, down the slope, through a hay meadow, to a second small sprung gate in a wall.

Continue ahead through another hay meadow (wall on your left) to a third small sprung gate. There is a PW four-finger signpost here directing you to turn left, rather than continuing directly to **Gayle** ¼ mile ahead. The fourth post points to Aysgill Force ½ mile away. Continue with a wall on your left, through a gate to a stile and a tarmac road. Turn right down the road for a short distance until you come to a stile and PW signpost on the left (**Gayle** ⅛ mile). Cross the stile and go half right on a flagged path, through a wooden sprung gate in front of a house boundary wall, then half left, on another flagged path, towards some houses, to reach a sprung gate in a wall, then to a road. (Note that there are curved stones set into the wall here which reduces the width of the gap; these seem quite common in this area.) Go ahead down a flagged path between the houses to another road. This is a housing estate in **Gayle**, a small hamlet adjacent to **Hawes**. Cross the road here and turn left on the pavement for a short distance, before reaching a PW signpost (FP **Hawes** ¼ ml). There are a few yards of tarmac (stone barn on the right) which takes you to a set of two wooden gates, (the first has 'push' on it and the second one 'pull') then a flagged path ascending to the right (wire fence on the right) called **Bealer Bank** which was used by packhorses in olden times.

The modern factory you pass on the left going into **Hawes** is the Wensleydale Creamery, the home of Wensleydale cheese, saved from extinction by Wallace and Grommit. You go over the mound to a squeeze gap in a wall (curved stones set into the gap). From here you can see **St Margaret's Church** in the near distance. The orange lichen on the wall either side of the squeeze stile, and the flagged path to the church, is very photogenic. Go down the flagged path to the church. At the end of this path is a PW signpost pointing back to **Gayle** (¼ mile). There are three wooden gates here. The large one on the right has a white acorn on the gatepost inviting you to go right. The middle, smaller wooden gate also takes you to the right. This will take you down a flagged path to the main street where you need to turn left for the main shops and pubs (and the youth hostel). If, however, you go through the left gate and follow the indicated flagged path and keep the church on your right, you will also come out into the main street of **Hawes** by means of a short enclosed passageway between two buildings. There is a PW finger post attached to the wall of the building on the left here saying '**Gayle Lane** ½ ML'. The PW continues on your right, but we are finished for the day.

Regarding the two paths either side of the church, I wonder if this is a deliberate attempt to create two lanes of traffic (it is less slippery in the wet if you go up via the stone passageway) for PW walkers travelling in opposite directions?

The public toilets are up the A684 road on your left. Just past the toilets is a chip shop, which, in my opinion, produces the best fish and chips on the Pennine Way. Further up, on the side of a hill, is the youth hostel, which was officially opened on 7 April 1973. One of the purpose built PW hostels. You should arrive in plenty of time to go to your accommodation, do shopping, laundry (which closes early), bank etc. All these are available in the market town of **Hawes** in Wensleydale. If you can afford the time, it is worth having a rest day here, as you won't see anything this big until you reach Middleton-in-Teesdale. You will feel better having a day without a pack on your back too.

Section 9 – Hawes to Keld

Distance – 12.4 miles / 19.9 km
Height gained on PW route – 675 m (2,215 ft)
Height lost on PW route – 630 m (2,067 ft)

Route outline: Hawes to Hardraw; Bluebell Hill; Great Shunner Fell; Thwaite; Kisdon House; Keld.

View back to Thwaite prior to ascent towards Doctor Wood

Section 9.1

Return to the passage leading to **St Margaret's Church**. Facing out, with your back to the passage, turn right, and walk down the **A684** road, past the post office on your right, round a bend as it curves to the left, and at the fork, where there is a fenced grassed area with various wooden carvings inside it, go down the minor road (i.e. away from the **A684**), past the **Old Station House**, to a road bridge over the dismantled railway line.

If you look over the wall, on the right, you will see the old railway station with an old steam train (number 67345) on a short section of track. The railway came to Hawes in 1878. There used to be a branch line from Garsdale, operated by the Midland Railway Company, and one to Leyburn, run by the North Eastern Railway Company. Alas the railway lines to Hawes closed in 1964, which is a shame as it would have been very useful to tourism and PW walkers now. Garsdale still has a railway station, so if you are walking the PW in sections, you can either walk the 7 miles along the road, or take The Little White Bus, to Garsdale which is on the Settle to Carlisle railway line.

Continue over the bridge to a PW signpost on the left (**Haylands Bridge** ¼ ml), where you go through a wooden gate then along a flagged path, passing a stone barn on the left. There is a wire fence to the left of the flagged path. At the end of the field, you go through a wooden kissing gate back to the road. Continue ahead on the road, which crosses the **River Ure** via **Haylands Bridge**, then along the road as it bends to the left, then uphill towards some trees. On the left, go up some concrete steps, to a small sprung wooden gate in the wall, next to a PW signpost (**Hardraw** ¾ ml). After the gate you continue ahead through a field with a dry stone wall on your left. At the end you go through the wooden field gate or use the wooden kissing gate next to it. Continuing in the same direction, with the wall still on your left, you go through another field to a second kissing gate. The next field exit is a gap in the wall ahead rather than a gate or stile. The path continues across the next field to a large wooden gate where you join up with a narrow flagged path that takes you to the hamlet of **Hardraw**, passing through three more wooden gates or stiles in the walls that cross your path. It is difficult to get lost here, as there is only the one flagged path between these two points.

Section 9.2

You emerge onto a road, at a PW signpost (**Hawes** 1¼ ml) with the Green Dragon Inn on your right.

If you want to see Hardraw Force, England's highest waterfall above ground, according to Wainwright, take the small detour to the Inn. There is a charge to see the waterfall (£2 in 2011). The Inn has a bunkhouse and also does camping.

The PW turns left along the road for a short distance to a PW sign-post on the right (**Thwaite** 8 ml) where you turn right up a track, with a wall on the left and a building on your right, heading towards a house in the near distance. This walled lane climbs **Hollin Hill**, and then bends left, past some trees, to climb **Bluebell Hill**. When the walled lane ends at a wooden gate, (there is a wooden ladder stile to the left of the gate) you continue ahead, into open countryside. Shortly, a minor track goes to the right (Hearne Coal Road). A finger post on the PW signpost here says it is also a Public Bridleway to Pickersett Nab. Do not take the minor track but continue on the main track (effectively the left fork). Further along, a path goes off left to Cotterdale by another signpost. Continue ahead uphill. A wall, which was on your far left, comes up to the track, before you reach **Little Fell**. It again meets the track by **Hearne Top**, where you go through a large wooden gate, with a ladder stile next to it. Shortly afterwards you meet a three-pointer PW signpost. Cotterdale is 2¼ miles ahead, **Hardraw** is 1¾ miles behind, and **Thwaite** is 6¼ miles up the track on your right.

You continue uphill on this track, heading NNW initially. There are cairns from time to time to guide you, but after about 10–15 minutes of walking, some newly laid slabs appear (2013) and there are the occasional small blue topped posts beside the path to guide you. In clear weather the route is quite visible as you are walking on a ridge that will take you to **Great Shunner Fell**. Just after a section of duck-boards, over the slight rise from **Black Hill Moss**, the path crosses a dried up streambed (which does flow after heavy rain).

> Pause here and have a look at the rocks that make up the streambed. There are peculiar markings that look like rows of deep dots in the stones. These are probably the fossilised remains of ancient ferns. Several of the boulders set in the track leading up to the stream also have fossilised ferns embedded in them.

The path continues northwards from here, with the surface sometimes a stoned path, sometimes slabbed and sometimes peat. There was a lot of relaying of slabs in 2013 as they had been sinking into the peat. The ascent seems endless. There is a slight climb up to **Crag End Beacon**, and then it levels off, and there are more newly laid slabs. Just before the next incline, which has flat cobble stones laid into the path, there are lots of yellow bog asphodel (in the summer). Women in the 16th century used these star shaped flowers to dye their hair yellow. It is about four miles from where you left the walled lane to reach the summit of **Great Shunner Fell**. Eventually, after the path swings to the NE, on a sandy path, a stone structure appears on the horizon ahead. This is a well-built cross-shaped shelter, with stone seats built into to it, and a cleverly disguised trig point at the end (S 7747).

> There is also a stone tablet built into the shelter next to the trig point with Wensleydale Round Table on it, and tucked into the shelter is a small plaque on a piece of slate relating to Robert Frizzell 1953 to 2013 'He loved life. He loved walking. He loved this path'. The cross-shelter enables walkers to have some protection from the elements here whatever the direction of the weather. In good weather it is an obvious boots off stop for lunch.

There is a fence around the summit of **Great Shunner Fell** and to reach the shelter and to leave it, you cross a wooden step stile in the fence on the ascent, and a new (2013) small wooden gate on the descent.

Section 9.3
You leave the summit shelter, heading NE down a flagged path to the small wooden gate in the wire fence. On the steep descent, shortly afterwards, the cobbles appear again. They are helpful in dry weather but take care when the weather is wet. Again, in good weather, the path is obvious as it is white(ish) and stands out quite well. From the cobbles you can see a small pool on the right of the path. You pass this shortly. Again the slabs depart and the going is sandy or peaty underfoot. Cairns line the route, a reminder that the weather isn't always sunny here and route finding can be difficult in inclement conditions. A couple of minutes after passing the pool, the path, which then descends, reaches a very tall well-built cairn (over six feet high). You now descend again down the slope and the slabs reappear. The path then levels out once again and soon afterwards you descend on the slabbed path to cross a short section of duckboards, which form a wooden bridge over the soft peat. The next section is a bit like the route over Featherbed Moss on day one as it weaves in and out of peat groughs. The slabbed path bends to the right then descends through a spoil heap to reach a walled lane accessed via a metal gate, to descend into **Thwaite**. The views ahead on the descent are delightful. Real picture postcard stuff! You pass two barns on the way down to the **B6270** at the end of the stony track. Here is a PW signpost informing you that **Hardraw** is 8 miles behind you.

Section 9.4
Turn right on the road and descend into the village of **Thwaite**. The famous Kearton Country Hotel and Coffee Shop is here so it is a great way to spend an hour or so if you can spare the time. They provide

accommodation too. Turn left, (away from the **B6270**), past the front of the hotel and continue ahead on a minor road which takes you to a narrow walled path, crossing two stiles. When you get to a third stile in a wall which crosses the path, turn left at the PW signpost. **Keld** is 3 miles away. The post also has wooden signs saying, 'No camping in fields' and 'Meadow land, single file'. Do not go ahead as that path goes to Muker, 1 mile distant. There is a helpful white painted PW and an arrow pointing left on a flagstone set into the ground ahead of you.

> You are now in Swaledale, which is a beautiful place of hay meadows and stone barns in the corner of almost every field. It is well worth getting the camera out here. You are now heading towards **Kisdon Hill**, where the path will climb along the edge towards the wooded area (**Doctor Wood**) half right ahead. Again, there are fine views here, both on the climb up and on the walk high above the River Swale.

Turn left towards a gap in the wall. There is no real path here but the line of the path is a different shade of green from the rest of the field. Pass through the gap and continue ahead in the same direction to cross a bridge over a tree-lined stream (**Skeb Skeugh**). The path now bends to the right and ascends another grassy field (wall on your right) to a stile in the corner of the field (PW signpost; see the photograph at the beginning of this section). Turn half right, uphill towards the corner of a wood ahead (**Doctor Wood**). This path cuts up the side of the hill through ferns and heather. There are good views back towards the village from here. You meet a wall on your right, and then go through a small gate (barn on your right), turning right to another gate in a wall, past another barn on your right. Go half right along a narrow stony path, then left, passing another stone barn, on your left, to a gate. Here you follow a wall round to the right (PW signpost on the corner) towards some buildings (**Kisdon House**) to another gate set in a wall ahead. Turn left (north), through another gate and enter a walled lane. At the end of the walled lane is a T-junction where **Keld** is to the left and Muker is to the right. Turn right on this lane for a few yards to a PW signpost where you turn left (northwards), past a barn, and ascend up the slope, crossing two stiles to meet a wall on the right. You are now on the higher slopes of **Kisdon Hill**. Cross three more stiles in the walls ahead that meet the wall on your right. After this the wall drops away and you continue ahead, on a grassy path, passing through gaps in three walls until you come to small sprung wooden gate in a wall.

As you are high above the River Swale, on the North Gang Scar, there are good views to your right. There was a lot of lead mining activity in this area in the past and the ruined buildings on the opposite slopes by the spoil heaps are Crackpot Hall.

The path continues around **Kisdon Hill**, to another sprung gate where it meets an old wall on the right. This stays on the right for about half a mile to where you will find a three-fingered PW signpost, which directs you, right (FP **Keld**), through a gap in the wall. After a short while you come to a T-junction and another three-fingered PW signpost, which informs you that you are now only ⅓ mile from **Keld**. Muker is 2¼ miles to the right. Turn left here along a good path. The next PW signpost tells you that you are now ⅕ mile from **Keld**. Such accuracy will never be repeated again on the Pennine Way! Continue ahead, through a gate, then on a wide track, to a footbridge on the right, over the **River Swale**.

You will need to make your way back to this point tomorrow, but your priority today is your bed for the night, so continue ahead to the village of **Keld**. There is a campsite (Park Lodge), plus Keld Bunkhouse and Park House Campsite, one B&B and Keld Lodge, (the old youth hostel), which is now a small licensed hotel. As **Keld** is also on Wainwright's Coast-to-Coast walk, which also competes for accommodation here, you are strongly advised to book ahead. **Keld** has <u>no mobile phone signal</u>, no pub, and no shops, but it does have a public telephone box and a public toilet.

If time permits, you can continue four miles further north on the PW to the famous **Tan Hill Inn**, which has a bunkhouse, B&B and a few wild camping pitches outside.

Section 10 – Keld to Baldersdale (via Clove Lodge or Bowes)

Distance – 14.2 miles / 22.8 km
Height gained on *Main PW route* – 475 m (1,558 ft)
Height lost on Main PW route – 460 m (1,509 ft)

Main Route outline: Keld to Tan Hill Inn; Sleightholme Moor; Sleightholme Farm; Trough Heads; God's Bridge; A66; Deepdale Beck; Race Yate; Clove Lodge.

Bowes Loop alternative outline: Keld to Tan Hill Inn; Sleightholme Moor; Sleightholme Farm; Trough Heads; East Mellwaters; Lady Myres; Bowes; West Stoney Keld; Levy Pool; Goldsborough; East Friar House; Blackton.

Note: The Bowes Loop is an extra 3.7 miles (5.9 km) but there is no extra height gained or lost by taking the Bowes Loop.

Sleightholme Moor – in a dry summer

Section 10.1

Make your way back from your overnight accommodation in **Keld** along the track (**Keld Lane**), to the three-pointer PW signpost and descend down the bridleway (trees on your left and wire fence on your right) to the footbridge over the **River Swale** that you passed yesterday on your way to **Keld**. Turn left, over the footbridge (don't go right, or you will be on Wainwright's Coast-to-Coast walk, which also passes through **Keld**), and ascend up the bank on the left, past another PW signpost, through a gate, passing between the buildings of **East Stonesdale Farm**. Continue ahead, uphill, through another gate, where you enter a walled lane for a short distance, with another gate at the end, and another PW signpost. Continue ahead then slightly left, past a barn on your left. When the wall on your left meets another wall ahead, go though the metal gate in the wall, then shortly through a gate in a wire fence which brings you to open country (**Black Moor**). The path continues along the ridge, (with Startindale Gill to the west), crossing two small streams before the path reaches **How Gill**. Here you pass through a gate in a wall ahead and join a farm track coming from Frith Lodge away to the right. Go ahead on the track, and when the track veers downhill to the left, continue ahead, past a barn, set in the stone wall now on your left, through a metal gate, to a walled enclosure with two barns inside (gates at the entrance and exit). As you leave the enclosure, there is a PW signpost just after a small stream, (**Mould Gill**), where a finger post points to the left, to a public bridleway (not the PW) which heads west, and then south to join the farm track from Frith Lodge.

The PW continues NNW and about 75 yards south of **Lad Gill**, it bends slightly right to the Gill, where you go through a small wooden gate and cross a stone (clapper) footbridge. Here the path ascends NE, then north, where it becomes a green track. It finally bends NE again towards **Tan Hill**. Ignore a path, which veers off left at a signpost. You should have your first sight of **Tan Hill Inn** around here.

Tan Hill Inn, the highest above sea level at 526 metres / 1,732 feet, was made famous by a double-glazing advert in the 1980s where a feather was dropped against an internal window when there was a stiff breeze outside, with the slogan, 'Fit the best. Everest'. It was also used in a werewolf film where it was the 'Wolf and Whistle'. Full details can be found on their excellent website. **Tan Hill Inn** is on the boundaries of Cumbria, Durham and North Yorkshire. Once it was on a junction of important packhorse trails. Coal was mined here using vertical bell-pits which have left their scars on the surrounding landscape.

The path dips into a peat channel, and there is a PW signpost just before it, and another shortly afterwards, directing you left down the track to the **Tan Hill Inn**. The PW signpost here says you are 4¼ miles from **Keld**.

In the early days of the PW the Inn was much smaller and it was a gloomy, peat-smoked place but the beer was good. These days it is light, airy, has accommodation (bunkhouse and B&B), good food and frequent entertainment many nights of the week. The beer is still good I am pleased to say. I have stayed there, but on a night when there was no entertainment. How noisy it gets when they have a live band is one for you to answer.

Section 10.2

You turn right along the road in front of the Inn for a few yards. Before you get to the cattle grid, at a PW signpost (**Bowes** 8 ml), go half left to a wooden step stile in a wooden fence.

This path starts off well and takes you across **Sleightholme Moor** with white-topped posts and the occasional cairn as your guide. In dry clear weather it is fine, although it can still be boggy underfoot in places, and sometimes you need to be careful not to lose the path. It used to be a place of dread in the early days of the Pennine Way so if you really can't take it, or there have been several days of heavy rain which will make the path very boggy, keep to the tarmac road (called the Long Causeway) for about two miles, and then at the fork, take a metalled road, left, (**Sleightholme Moor Road**), which will bring you back to the PW.

The path is on peat and heads NE, close to the Long Causeway for a while, but when the road bends to the right, the PW continues in the same direction to meet **Coal Gill Sike**, which flows into **Frumming Beck**. Once upon a time it crossed the beck but it has since been rerouted so that it remains on the northern side where the ground is better drained and firmer. There are white-topped posts to help you navigate this section of the route. You will see one on the grassy descent to the sike. The path is quite boggy after that for a while, before it returns to firmer ground.

The first major landmark to keep an eye open for is a stone circular sheepfold on the right near the path. The next landmark is a wooden plank (duckboards) bridge with a guidepost (yellow directional arrow) by it and a nice conical shaped cairn a few yards further on. If you look back, **Tan Hill Inn** should be quite visible in a dip with a small conical hill on its right. The path bends slightly more to the right here (**Frumming Beck** still on your right) and continues in that direction until it eventually hits a track. However, before this, your next landmark is to cross two plank (duckboards) bridges next to each other, then there is a longer section of duckboards, then a small duckboard bridge with a white topped post next to it, then two more duckboards a few minutes apart, one with two sheepfolds visible on your right. After this, you just keep plodding on until the track appears on the right, ahead. When you get to the track, turn right on it and cross **Frumming Beck** using a new metal bridge (painted green in 2011). This track will take you to the **Sleightholme Moor Road**, which meets the track from the right. On the way you will pass a small section of wall with ten new shooting butts (2013) running parallel with the track. At the junction there is a PW signpost (**Tan Hill** 3¼ miles and **Trough Heads** 2 miles). Turn left along the road, which is part of cycle route 20 (W2W). If you want softer walking there is a grass verge alongside the road.

Section 10.3

Sleightholme Moor Road is little more than a tarmac track itself but it takes you to a metal gate across it, above **Sleightholme Farm**. Look out for an old pretty circular sheepfold by a footbridge on the way. There is a good photo opportunity on the hill before the gate too. At the gate you enter a walled lane, which takes you to the farm and its substantial barns. The farm had a 'For Sale' sign in August 2012 but it is still occupied (2013). On a stone gatepost on the left is the word 'BULL' painted on it in white. This is a timely reminder that there is usually a bull in that field but fortunately for us, the PW does not enter that particular field. Shortly after the farm is a stone bridge (**Jack Shields Bridge**) with a large tree next to it on the left. Ahead, the building on the right is **Kingdom Lodge**, (another 'For Sale' sign next to it in 2013) which used to be a barn in Wainwright's day. Shortly after the lodge is a PW signpost on the left (**Tan Hill** 4½ miles), with 'Public Bridleway' carved vertically into the post, and this directs you left, through a large wooden gate in the wall. Follow the field path, down the slope through two more gates to **Intake Bridge**. This has gates at both ends to prevent farm animals roaming. Go up the grassy slope around the hill ahead, away from **Sleightholme Beck** to a wall. Turn right and walk beside the wall until you come to a large wooden gate, next to a wooden post with a yellow disc on it. Go through the gate, turn right and continue with the wall now on your right. Ahead, is **Trough Heads Farm** and a PW signpost. Here you need to make a decision because **Bowes** is straight ahead, and **God's Bridge** and the **A66** is to the left.

Main route to Baldersdale / Clove Lodge

Original PW signpost at Clove Lodge

Section 10.4

If you are heading for **God's Bridge** and **Clove Lodge**, turn left at the signpost to cross **Wytham Moor**.

The path across the peaty moor has white-topped posts to aid navigation. Before you reach a wall, you should be able to see, ahead, the busy **A66** Brough to Bowes road. In Wainwright's day it was a busy road and you crossed it with care from a stile on one side, to another on the other side. Now it is a dual carriageway with a crash barrier in the middle, and crossing it requires other methods. You should also be able to see a white track going up the hill from some buildings (**Rock Bridge Cottages**). You will walk up the track and pass by the cottages on your way to the **A66**.

The path over the moor initially goes slightly north of NW, then it swerves to the right, round a bank and into a brook, then left again, to follow a wall on the right to a gate. From here, if you look back along the wall, you should be able to see **Bowes Castle** in the far distance. Go through the gate (another wall on your right) to descend, northwards, towards **Rock Bridge Cottages** and an old limekiln on the hillside below them. At the bottom of the hill you cross a small limestone pavement, which has a pool of water below it. This is called **God's Bridge**, for obvious reasons. If the weather is nice, it is a good place to rest and air your feet. Head for the track and go through a metal gate. The track passes between the buttresses of a dismantled railway bridge (opened in 1861 by the South Durham and Lancashire Union Railway and carried mainly coal and iron ore. It was closed in 1962) and climbs up the hill towards the **A66**. When the track bends sharp right, turn left at the PW sign-post (**God's Bridge** ¼ mile and **Clove Lodge** 3¾ miles) by the wall beneath the raised bank of the **A66**. Note the blue chevrons on the signpost. This denotes that you are on a bridleway. Here there is another metal painted sign pointing left, which says, 'Pennine Way via underpass 200 metres'.

Turn left to a wooden gate (next to a large metal gate), then turn right to another large metal gate and go under the **A66** ahead of you via a round, metal lined tunnel. After the tunnel you go right, up the slope to a gate, then ahead on a green grassy track, parallel with the **A66**, to another PW signpost by the wooden fence (**God's Bridge** ½ mile, **Clove Lodge** 3½ miles). You have come three corners round a rectangle to get to where you are now. In front of you is a building (**Pasture End**). Walk past to the left of the building and follow the wall north to the wall corner where a signpost directs you half right across the moor. There is a short guidepost with a white acorn on it further on to help you keep to the path. There is also the occasional cairn. You cross **Rove Gill** and head NNW on a good peaty path, passing a pile of stones on the left, little bigger than some cairns you may have passed, with the rather ambitious name of **Ravock Castle**!

Ravock Castle used to be an old shepherd's hut and in the 1960s you could make out the wall foundations, but there is nothing left now. There is a nice black and white photograph of it in Chris Wright's book.

From here, because you are on the highest point before descending into **Deepdale Beck**, there are good views to the ridge ahead. The PW runs to the left of a long wall going over the ridge in the distance. Before that, by another cairn, you should be able to see a large dark brown cabin, which is a tea hut for shooters with the addition of a useful shelter at one end, which is open to all walkers. It makes a useful place for a rest out of the weather. If you have a monocular, or a good zoom lens, you might be able to pick out **Tan Hill Inn** in the far distance behind you (if the weather is clear).

The path descends to **Duckett Sike**, which is crossed by means of breeze blocks set into the ground. Continue your descent to the wide track ahead. This runs east to west and has the brown hut with the shelter in it.

Head for, and cross, the wooden footbridge (railings on both sides) over **Deepdale Beck**, then bear left to the wooden gate in the wall. Go through the gate and, with the wall on your right, begin the long ascent over **Knotts Hills**. The path can be a bit faint in places but you can't really get lost because of the wall on your right. Cross **Knotts Sike** on the way up. At the top, (**Race Yate**) go through the gate in the wooden fence, next to the PW signpost. This has two finger posts, pointing north and south, which have 'Pennine Way' on each one. The reservoir, visible ahead on the left is **Balderhead Reservoir**.

Continue ahead, over the fairly flat terrain of **Cotherstone Moor**. Go past a signpost, cross **Duck Sike**, then later cross a feeder to **Burners Sike**, then begin the gradual descent to the tarmac road ahead, where there is a PW signpost (**Pasture End** 3⅓ miles).

Turn left on the road, past a small car park and round a bend to the right, to reach a wooden gate. Directly ahead is **Clove Lodge**, which does B&B, and has a bunkhouse, and allows camping for a reasonable fee.

The owners had the Lodge up for sale at the end of 2012 (and it remained unsold in 2013). If they do sell, hopefully the new owners will continue to do B&B and maintain the bunkhouse. You should check before you leave for the PW, as the alternative is to use the Bowes Loop, or walk to **Tan Hill** instead of **Keld** and then make your way to **Middleton-in-Teesdale**, which has plenty of accommodation. The bunkhouse is the first building on the left in the courtyard. Note the tree on the road in front of it. Nailed to it is a very old PW finger post that has been there for many many years (see the photograph at the end of section 10.3).

Bowes Loop alternative to Baldersdale / Clove Lodge

Junction at road on route to West Stoney Keld

Section 10.5 (Alternative)

From **Trough Heads**, continue ahead with the wall on your right. When the wall bends to the left (PW signpost with a blue chevron) go left with it passing a large wooden gate in the wall on your right (don't go through it), to reach a wooden gate in the wall ahead. Go through the gate (wall still on your right) and descend to another wooden gate, where you meet a grassy green track. Go left on the track for a short distance to meet a gravel farm track, (West Mellwaters Farm is up the track on your left). Go right along the track and cross a cattle grid. You will shortly go through a gate and over a second cattle grid (**East Mellwaters Farm** immediately on your right) to reach a tarmac track. At this T-junction, turn left down the tarmac road for a short distance until you come to a cattle grid. Just past the cattle grid is a stone bridge over the **River Greta**. Don't cross the cattle grid or the bridge but go right through a small wooden gate in the wall on your right. There is a PW signpost with a yellow chevron here, which says **Bowes** is 1¾ mile ahead. In front of you is a narrow cinder path with trees and the **River Greta** on your left. Follow this, through a gate in a wall ahead. With a wall now on your right, the cinder path takes you to a substantial wooden footbridge with stone steps up to it (**Cardwell Bridge**) over **Sleightholme Beck**. Aim for the left of the building ahead (**West Charity Farm**), passing under power lines in the field as you do so. At the farm track (PW signpost) go right, through a metal gate, then left (another PW signpost) around the bend, leaving the farmyard, soon crossing a cattle grid in the track, over a concrete bridge across a stream, and finally through a metal gate in a wall across the track.

Go past **Lady Myres Farm** (on the right). Shortly afterwards, look out for a PW signpost with a yellow chevron on the left (**Bowes** ¾ mile), next to a large wooden gate in a dry stone wall. You should also be able to see the footbridge over the **River Greta** too. Head for the footbridge, through the small wooden gate in front of it, climb the concrete steps and cross the green painted metal-based bridge. Bear right along a faint path on the grass then left to enter a walled lane with **Swinholme Farm** on your right. Go past the farm, through a gate and downhill on a sunken lane to a PW signpost on the right by a stile. The finger post pointing back towards the way you have just come says '**River Greta** ⅓ mile'. Go over the wooden step stile (acorn on the left post), and across a shallow gully to a stone step stile with a sprung wooden gate in the wall ahead. Cross this and after a few yards, go over a wooden step stile in a four-bar wooden fence. Continue ahead, in the same direction to cross another wooden step stile in a fence next to a tree. You next go over a stone step stile in a wall next to two trees and continue eastwards with **Bowes Castle** in sight on the left. Go over another stone step stile and pass **Bowes Castle** on your left. Go through a metal gate on your left, then through a wooden gate next to a PW signpost with yellow chevrons, to reach the road.

Bowes has a Roman fort (Lavatris), and the castle, built within the northwest corner of the fort, is Norman. The keep, that you see, dates back to the late 1100s. You may already know a little about **Bowes** because Dotheboys Hall in Nicholas Nickleby was based on a school in **Bowes** run by William Shaw, which Dickens visited in 1838. You pass this on the left just before you turn right to cross over the **A66**.

Section 10.6 (Alternative)

Turn left on the road, passing **Bowes Castle** again, to a T-junction, where you turn left. (The Ancient Unicorn is to the right if you have booked in there.) At the fork in the road, go right up the road, to cross over the busy **A66**. Continue ahead, up the hill, passing some allotments on the right. Ignore a road (**Clint Lane**) on the right (with a WT tower), unless you have booked B&B there. Continue along the tarmac road, passing the foundations of old Air Ministry buildings.

These building were once used to store poisonous gas and other nasty items. There are a profusion of warning signs along the road, but fortunately the cattle, which have grazed in these fields for years can't read, as they blissfully ignore the signs.

You later pass a farm track on the right (to East Stoney Keld Farm). Soon after, look out for a PW signpost on the left next to a stone step stile with sprung gate in the wall. The finger post pointing back says '**Bowes** 1¼ miles' (see photograph at end of section 10.4).

The next small section of the PW cuts off a corner in the road. The path is quite overgrown which seems to indicate that a lot of PW walkers keep to the road, which is both faster and easier underfoot.

Cross the stile and head half left across scrubland, to the right of a large stone barn. Cross two stone step stiles in the walls ahead and a third stone step stile with a solid sprung gate on top. There is a round green waymark on one post. Descend down rough pasture to **Stonykeld Spring**, which is a stone structure, which looks like a rectangle with a dome at one end. Go up the slope, past a wall corner, and then head for the wooden gate and PW signpost to reach **West Stoney Keld Farm**. Turn right on the track (PW signpost) and go through the metal farm gate (here is another PW signpost informing you that **Bowes** is now 2 miles behind and **Goldsborough** is 2½ miles ahead) where you turn left to rejoin a farm track for **Levy Pool**.

Section 10.7 (Alternative)

You soon go through a metal gate, over a cattle grid, to arrive at the substantial group of buildings which form the **Levy Pool** farmstead. Here you go through a second gate, and cross **Deepdale Beck** via a large footbridge which has several stone steps (with wooden hand rails on both sides) both onto and off the footbridge. Here care is needed to avoid losing the path. In clear weather, you should be able to see some white-topped posts and the path up the slope ahead.

It is worse for PW walkers coming the other way as there are two paths over **Hazelgill Rigg** to the north of you and it is very easy to take the wrong one. The only good point is that they both end up at the same place, the footbridge.

You should bear right along the beck for a few yards before heading NE up the slope to (hopefully) a guidepost with a white acorn. Turn half left, then northwards, past a few more guideposts, to reach **Hazelgill Beck**, where you go left, cross the beck, then half right up the bank, before heading NE through the bracken to reach a track, which crosses ahead. Turn right on the track to reach a sandstone wall. Turn left with the wall on your right. It later changes to a fence, then back to a wall again. There are numerous signs on the other side of the wall which say 'Military Firing Range. Keep out when warning flags or lights are displayed'. You cross **Blackpool Sike** then **Hare Sike**, and then pass what looks like the corner of a ruined building built into the wall. Here the path leaves the wall as you go through a metal gate and head slightly west of NW across rough pasture towards a wooden guidepost with **Goldsborough Hill**, a very distinctive flat gritstone-topped hill, in the background. You will soon reach a black metal footbridge over **Yawd Sike**, which you cross. You now head towards the left slopes of **Goldsborough**, clearly visible in fine weather, and then descend to a tarmac road and PW signpost which tells you that **Levy Pool** is 2½ miles behind. The reservoir that you could see on your descent to the road is **Blackton Reservoir. Clove Lodge** is ¾ mile to the left on the road and Cotherstone is 5 miles to the right.

The Bowes Loop shuns the direct route along the road to **Clove Lodge**, but if it is your overnight stop, the cross country Bowes Loop route meets the PW main route on the grassy track to the north of the Lodge, so you will need to double back on the main route to reach it. Alternatively, you could just turn left along the road to the Lodge and retrace your steps the following morning. Do check and book your accommodation at **Clove Lodge** in advance if it is your intention to stay there.

Section 10.8 (Alternative)

Turn left on the road for a short distance, to a PW signpost (**Blackton Bridge** 1½ miles) then turn right onto the farm road to **East Friar House**, and over a cattle grid. When the track bends to the right, just before the farm, walk straight ahead through two small wooden gates. The first gate has a white acorn and yellow directional arrow and you walk ahead (wall on your left) towards a stone barn to the second gate. After the wall corner, turn left over a stone step stile. You now go through a series of six fields (wall on your left) with six stiles in the walls that cross your path. You should be able to see **Blackton Reservoir** on your right. The first stile is a stone step stile next to a metal farm gate. Next comes two stone step stiles over walls, then another stone step stile next to a metal farm gate. There is a yellow directional arrow on a post next to it and an acorn carved into the post. You now cross a small sike, go over a stone step stile then head for the corner of a wire fence where there is a short guidepost next to the corner fencepost. Descend down the slope towards a small gap in the trees to reach a grassy footbridge over **How Sike**. There is a metal field gate across the exit. Go up the slope to a stone step stile in the wall ahead with a sprung wooden gate on top and wooden marker post with a yellow directional arrow on it. Bear slightly left, down a gentle slope, through a hay meadow to a stone step stile (PW signpost – Bowes Loop) to reach a track. Here you will need to turn right to take you to **Blackton Bridge** and the PW, or, if you are heading to **Clove Lodge** for the night, turn left on the track (heading SSE), passing a ruined barn with noticeable rounded end walls, to reach **Clove Lodge.**

Kinder Downfall

Featherbed Moss in the High Peak

On the approach to Laddow Rocks

Ordnance Survey column at Blackstone Edge

Stoodley Pike from Coldwell Hill

Malham Cove

High Force, River Tees

High Cup Nick after heavy rain

Sycamore Gap on Hadrian's Wall

Rapishaw Gap where the PW leaves Hadrian's Wall

Descending from Windy Gyle

The Cheviot from the Border Ridge

Section 11 – Baldersdale (Clove Lodge) to Langdon Beck

Distance – 14.9 miles / 24 km
Height gained on PW route – 475 m (1,559 ft)
Height lost on PW route – 400 m (1,313 ft)

Route outline: Clove Lodge to Low Birk Hat; Mickleton Moor; How Farm; Grassholme Reservoir; Grassholme Farm; B6276; Wythes Hill Farm; B6277; Middleton-in-Teesdale (off route); Seaberry Bridge; Low Force; High Force; Cronkley Farm; Langdon Beck Bridge.

Looking back to Cronkley Farm from near Cronkley Bridge

Section 11.1

From the courtyard of **Clove Lodge** turn right, up the grassy track to a wooden gate and go through it. After a short while the track descends, towards a stone bridge, with **Blackton Reservoir** clearly visible ahead on the right.

What looks like a grassy slope on the hillside opposite **Blackton Reservoir** is in fact the dam of another reservoir (**Balderhead Reservoir**). The group of buildings in its shadow (with red doors) is Blackton, initially a farm, then a ruin, then an Outdoors Pursuit Centre, and on 26 April 1981 it became Baldersdale youth hostel. Unfortunately, it is now a management training centre and only available if you book the entire building which would be rather expensive. Another sad reminder of a hostel lost to walkers in an area of limited accommodation.

As you descend the track from **Clove Lodge** you will pass the ruins of an old barn, which judging by the remains, once had a curved roof. You pass by a stone step stile in the wall where the **Bowes Loop** path rejoins the main Pennine Way. Go through a metal gate across the track and cross a bridge over **Hunder Beck**, into a walled lane. This leads to a second bridge (**Blackton Bridge**) over a larger feeder (**River Balder**) into the reservoir. Wainwright considered this to be the halfway point of the PW.

The track bends right and goes up a grassy slope to an old metal gate near **Low Birk Hat**. There is a wooden PW sign on the gate. Go through the gate to the farmstead where Hannah Hauxwell used to live. By the buildings is a PW signpost directing you left up a tarmac road, over two cattle grids and up the slope past **Hannah's Meadow**, a rare example of a traditional northern hay meadow and a Site of Special Scientific Interest. There is a boardwalk going off to the left (ignore). The buildings at the end of the meadow are High Birk Hatt. Continue up the slope on the road, over another cattle grid to a wooden gate in the wall ahead, leading to a T-junction and another road. There is a PW signpost here informing you that you have travelled 1 mile since **Clove Lodge**. From the elevated position of the road, you get a good viewpoint (SE) towards **Goldsborough** hill in the distance.

Turn left on the road for a few yards, until you come to a PW signpost on the right, (**Grassholme Reservoir** 1¾ miles) next to a stone step stile in the wall. Go over this, to step down onto one of the many PW people counters on the route (although this one looks like it has seen better days).

> People counters are an important part of measuring walker usage on the path, so please do not abuse them. Ahead the path goes through a series of rough pasture and meadows, over a small hill, to a reservoir. After rain it can be a bit boggy in places but in dry weather you will wonder what all the fuss was about. The path is quite visible on the ground, with a dry stone wall on your right for the first half mile or so.

Cross **Hunder Sike** by means of four concrete blocks laid into the ford. Go ahead up the slope to a stile in a fence, next to a metal gate, cross a second stream (**Rokehole Sike**) and, with the wall still on your right, continue up the slope to a stone step stile in a cross wall ahead. Here you head slightly right to a second stone step stile, which you cross. The wall is now on your left and you cut across the corner of the field, passing a large guidepost on your right, to another stone step stile in the wall ahead, to the left of a wooden farm gate.

> Looking at the line walked on the ground, most walkers are oblivious of the large guidepost, away to the right in the rough pasture, as they seem to keep close to the wall along most of this field, veering to the right to reach the stile towards the end.

This stile has a small sprung gate at the top. Head to the right of the barn directly in front of you, (wall on your left), to cross a second stone step stile with another small sprung gate on top. There is a sign on the gate, which says, 'Please keep to the path and walk in single file'. This is to protect the hay meadow ahead. You now walk down a slight incline in the meadow, half right to a metal gate / gap in the wall on the right. Pass through this and head towards the farm buildings ahead to another metal gate. From here curve half left to a metal gate in the wall, next to a PW signpost. The finger post (**Blackton Bridge** 2¼ miles) points back towards the path you have just walked.

Section 11.2

Turn right on the tarmac road, passing **How Farm** on your left (barn on your right). Immediately past the farm, at a PW signpost (**Grassholme Farm** ½ mile) go left, through a wooden gate. Walk diagonally across a field, towards some trees, over a wooden step stile in a four-bar wooden fence, passing under the trees, through a small wooden gate, to descend (wall on your right) to a stone step stile in the right hand corner of the field. Ahead is the stone bridge carrying the tarmac road over **Grassholme Reservoir** (it makes a good photograph in sunny weather). Cross the stone step stile and head towards the PW signpost and a gap in the stone wall ahead. Here you climb another stone step stile in the wall to reach the tarmac road. The PW signpost (**Blackton Bridge** 2½ miles) directs you left down a steep hill to the road bridge, which you cross. By the metal railings on the right there is a car park which the local fishermen use, and an old PW map board. Continue up the road towards **Grassholme Farm**.

Note that on a gate by a barn is a green sign with yellow lettering which says 'No path through meadow. Right of Way (Pennine Way) through farmyard 100 metres'. This relates to a time (Wainwright page 77) when the PW went diagonally across the field to a stile rather than through the farmyard.

Turn right into the farmyard at the PW signpost with a yellow chevron (**Wythes Hill** 1 mile). Go through the farm gate on the other side and descend on a farm track, before going left, at a tall guidepost with a yellow directional arrow and an acorn carved into it, down a dip, then up towards an obvious gap in the wall ahead, to a stone step stile, (small guidepost with carved acorn to the right of it and a ruined barn about 100 yards further to the right).

Cross the stile and continue up the slope to a gate in a wall (large barn slightly off route on the left). Go through the gate, down a slight slope (wall on your left) to a small plank bridge over a sike, and up a slope to a stile in the wall ahead. Cross the stile, go down into a dip, through a gap in an old wall (roofless barn on your right), then bear right towards the Nissen hut that you would have seen from the top of the hill. You should reach the road (**B6276**) by the Nissen hut where you cross over a stone step stile in the wall by a PW signpost (**Grassholme Farm** ½ mile [yellow chevron] and **Middleton-in-Teesdale** 2½ miles [blue chevron]). Directly ahead of you is the farm road to **Wythes Hill Farm**. Go up the road, passing the Nissen hut on the right, to the farm. Here a lovely sign with a sheep's head in the middle, directs you left, away from the farm, down a gravelled track, past a new stone house and other buildings on the right. Look out for a short guidepost on the left, with a white acorn on it and a yellow directional marker. Go down a walled track, which ends at a metal gate just after you cross **Carl Beck**. Go through the gate, and go across (uphill) a field towards some rushes in the top left of the field, in front of a stone step stile in the wall. The stones on either side of the gap at the top are painted white but it can still be quite hard to spot sometimes. There should also be a yellow directional arrow on a post next to it.

This next section is quite complex and it can be easy to get 'misplaced' so care should be taken with route finding from here into **Middleton-in-Teesdale**. After the white-topped stile, go diagonally right across the field to another stile / gap in a wall. From here you continue in the same direction to meet a track coming in from the right. Turn left on the track to a metal gate. Go through the gate, and turn right with the track (wall on your right). Continue ahead on the track, through a metal gate in the wall ahead, through a second metal gate in another wall ahead, (with a stone stile next to it but it is easier to use the gate), passing a roofless barn on your right after the second gate.

Continue in the same direction to another wall and go through the metal gate (stile next to it). Now go part left, passing below a walled plantation (**Pin Gate**) on the slope above (**Harter Fell**) on your left, to another gate and stile in the wall ahead. Here go half left, over a broken stone wall, past a (collapsed) cairn on the left. Here the path seems to fork, so ensure you take the left fork, down the slope, to a metal gate in a wall ahead, then to another gate. There should be a small stone building with a corrugated roof to your left, about fifty yards away. Go through the gate, and through another metal gate in a wall.

> This wall leads to a walled plantation on a hill, (away on your right), called Kirkcarrion, which is quite a prominent landmark in the area. A Bronze Age burial mound was excavated there in 1804.

Descend NE down a broad grassy slope to a metal gate in a wire fence with a stile next to it. Next to the stile are two thin vertically moveable pieces of wood, to allow dogs through. Behind you is Kirkcarrion, ahead, **Middleton-in-Teesdale** should now be visible. Continue ahead in the same direction for a short while. The path then bends left to meet a metal gate in a wall. Go through the gate and descend down the grassy slope to a track, which used to be the site of an old mineral railway. Cross the track and bear left down the slope to a wooden gate and PW signpost with a blue chevron (**Wythes Hill** 2¼ miles) with some cottages on the other side of the tarmac lane in front of you. On the other side of the gate is a 'Bull in field' sign, but I have yet to see one there.

Section 11.3

Turn right down the lane to meet the **B6277**. Turn left here, down the hill, passing Daleview Caravan Park (camping pitches available) on your right. Just before the cattle market, the PW turns left up a track, prompted by a PW signpost (**Low Force** 3½ miles).

Please bear in mind that **Middleton-in-Teesdale** is the only shopping point between here and **Alston**, two days ahead. There are pubs, cafés, a large Co-op store here, a post office, fish and chips, a bank (Barclays), and of course B&Bs. It is just too good to miss!

To reach **Middleton-in-Teesdale**, go down the road, over the road bridge over the **River Tees**. Turn right at the junction for the Co-op, keep ahead for the bank and chippie. The post office is by the junction. Once you have done all your shopping, retrace your steps back to the cattle market.

There used to be a railway station in Middleton but alas, it closed to passengers on 30 November 1964, before the PW was opened (the site of the station is now the Caravan Park). The next section of the PW is along the **River Tees**. In good weather it is well worth lingering so that you can fully enjoy the scenery. The only down side is that there is a barbed wire topped fence on some sections (so mind your expensive waterproofs) and the trees to the right of the path on some sections need some pruning, as you have to constantly duck under overhanging branches. It can be especially awkward if you have a tent or sleeping mat on the top of your rucksack.

The start of the walk is along a good track. You may see locals walking their dogs here. Go through two gates in quick succession (wall on your right) then ahead to another gate with a barn on the right. The fourth gate has a 'bull in the field' notice on it, (again I have yet to see it) which you go through. The path then goes over a stream (a couple of trees on your left and another barn on your right). When the wall on the right comes to an end, go though a metal gate on your left (stile next to it) and follow the wire fence on your right, (curved wall on your left) to a stone step stile. You go through a kissing gate shortly after. The next section of the PW takes you along the fields with the Tees on your right and the road on your left. The wall on your left is soon joined by a parallel wall on the right, forming an old lane for a short period. In a couple of places the Tees loops away to the right only to come back again. You cross several stone step stiles and a metal ladder stile, and two streams the second of which is **Crag Scar Force**.

The first real landmark is a barn on your left followed by two stone step stiles after which you go up a grassy slope to a substantial wooden step stile set in the corner of a fence. This is where you leave the open fields for a while as you will now have a wire fence on your left and trees on your right. Route finding is quite easy from here on. The path is well above the river now but after about a quarter of a mile you descend to a concrete bridge with metal railings, at **Rowton Beck**. Go over the wooden step stile at the end of the bridge and ahead to a second beck. This one is crossed via stepping-stones. You are now back at river level. Go over a wooden step stile in the wire fence ahead and continue with the fence on your left and the Tees on your right. The path curves left with the river, past a mounted lifebelt, past a barn on the left in the field, over three stiles, under power cables and finally through a wooden kissing gate in a wall ahead, to reach **Scoberry Bridge**.

Scoberry Bridge is a narrow three span wooden bridge, built in 1971, (replacing an earlier bridge) with wrought iron trestles. The bridge provides pedestrian access to Newbiggin over the river.

Section 11.4

Do not go over the bridge but continue ahead with the river still on your right. Cross a stream using three concrete blocks. There is a Natural England sign further along informing you that you are in Moor House National Nature Reserve. Soon after, go over a stile, ahead and over a wooden footbridge with wooden railings on both sides. Continue along the path to reach **Wynch Bridge**.

Wynch Bridge is a metal suspension bridge with a wooden lined base over the Tees, which gives pedestrian access to the B6277 road and Bowlees. Holwick lead miners originally used the bridge to get to a lead mine at Little Eggleshope. Surprisingly, this bridge was built in 1830 and was strengthened in 1992.

There is a four-finger signpost here. **High Force** is 1½ miles ahead, Bowlees Visitor Centre is 550 yards over the bridge (toilets are 750 yards), and Holwick is 1 mile to the left. Again, don't cross the bridge but keep to the left side of the river. The path is good underfoot here. The next highlight is two stone sheep on top of a sloping dry stone wall.

Carved in the stone beneath the sheep is *'A wonderful place to be. A walker'*. I am not too keen on sculptures in the countryside but this one by Keith Alexander is particularly well done and nice to look at. As you pass it by, if you look back, you will see a second inscription on the other *side 'It reverts to scrub. Once it's gone, it's lost. A farmer'*.

Next, on the right is **Low Force**. Not as spectacular as **High Force**, further up the Tees, but a nice place to rest a while nevertheless if you need a break. Continue ahead, through a wooden gate, on a nice flat path with a wire fence on your left and the Tees close by on the right. You cross a double plank bridge in the path passing a rocky island close to the river bank. After a section of slabs you pass through three more wooden gates to reach another bridge (**Holwick Head Bridge**, rebuilt in 1998) on the right.

> **Holwick Head Bridge** has a green painted girder base, with a column in the middle of the river supporting it, and a metal gate across the entrance.

Again don't cross the bridge as it takes you up through some trees to the High Force Hotel (and the B6277). Instead, continue up the slope of **Keedholm Scar**, through the juniper bushes, through a kissing gate.

> In 2012 the juniper bushes were attacked by a disease called *Phytotophthora austocedrae* and walkers had to wash their boots as they passed through the area.

The path levels off and goes through two more kissing gates. Shortly after, look out for a path branching off to the right through the bushes, as this will lead you to a great viewing point for the **High Force** waterfall.

> **High Force** is not the highest waterfall in England (Hardraw Force drops about 100 feet) but its drop of about 70 feet can be quite spectacular after a few days of very heavy rain. When there has been heavy rain, two waterfalls can occasionally spring from the top, one on either side. This is rare now following the building of a dam at **Cow Green** reservoir further up the Tees. W.A. Poucher, in his book, (*The Peak & Pennines* 1974 p380), said that this was a difficult subject to photograph because of the lighting and I agree with him. I have taken dozens of photographs here over the years but have never felt that I have really done it justice. Recently this natural viewing platform has had some of the obstructive vegetation cleared so it is at least less dangerous to get a reasonable photograph.

Retrace your steps back to the PW and continue up the slope to pass the waterfall on your right. The path levels off now. You continue along a gravel path, through a kissing gate, along the tranquil banks of the Tees. A sign that this may be disrupted is literally that. You will see a sign warning that blasting may occur between 11 am and 5 pm. On the right, across the river, in Dine Holm Scar, appears a large stone quarry, complete with tall industrial buildings. Again, like the one at **Horton-in-Ribblesdale**, this has been here for many, many, years and will stay until its licence runs out or the company goes out of business. So if you hear a continuous siren, they will be blasting.

As you get level with the quarry, you cross a footbridge over **Blea Beck**. This is a narrow concrete footbridge with five stone steps up to it and metal railings. After a few yards you cross a wooden step stile in the wooden / wire fence ahead. A fenced enclosure on the right protects a small nursery of trees. Continue ahead on the river-bank. A couple of hundred yards further upstream you cross a second footbridge with two stone steps, up in a fenced-off area of bushes. A narrow stony path around a stream takes you to a third footbridge with eight stone steps up to the footbridge. Shortly afterwards a short section of wooden sleepers appear, with chicken wire on top to prevent walkers slipping in the wet weather. These seem a bit of overkill in the summer though. You start your ascent up the slope, with a wire fence away on your left, and a closer one on your right. Then slabs reappear, then a plank bridge and more slabs as you go up **Bracken Rigg**. The PW becomes a wide grassy path with a wire fence reappearing on your left. The remains of a corrugated iron shed also litters the hillside. At the top is a stone marker with 'PW' and a directional arrow carved into it. The 'W' is very rounded. You should be able to see the path ahead from here, flagstones to the left of a stone wall. The flags descend into a dip, where you cross over a wooden step stile in a wire fence, and then the flagstones ascend up the slope with the wall on your right, to a gate. Continue ahead on the flagstones (wall on your right) down the slope towards an area of scrub. Keep a sharp look out for a small stile in the wall on the right, as you need to go over it. It has a wooden sprung gate in front of it and a short guidepost with a yellow arrow on it.

After you go through the gate, you descend on a grassy path, past another stone PW marker to a metal gate in a fence. Ahead you should be able to see a large wooden barn at **Cronkley Farm**. Bear left to another metal gate, then ahead, with a wall on your right and a wire fence on your left, to another gate. The PW used go between the buildings (PW signpost saying **High Force** 1¾ miles behind you) to reach a farm track, but you now have to follow a permissive path around the large wooden barn to reach the farm track. Follow this, down the slope to **Cronkley Bridge** where there is a three-fingered PW signpost (one pointing to the PW behind you, a second for the PW going ahead over the bridge, and a third for a footpath to **Maize Beck**; see photograph at beginning of this section).

Section 11.5

Turn right over the bridge crossing the **River Tees**. After you cross the bridge there is a second PW signpost, which directs you along the banks of the Tees (which is now on your left).

> In the summer, the hay meadows around the Tees are awash with colour. They are deliberately not cut until the seeds have fallen, guaranteeing the same glorious sight the following year. If you have B&B booked at The Dale in Forest-in-Teesdale, you need to leave the PW here and follow the footpath signs. Return here the following day to continue your walk.

Your first landmark is a small wooden gate in the wire fence, which drops down from the slope on your right. Go through this and continue ahead, with the Tees close to you on the left, and the grassy bank on your right. Not long after, the river forks. The left fork is the

River Tees, which you will see again tomorrow. You continue ahead alongside **Langdon Beck**, now on your left. On the opposite bank, just ahead, is a whitewashed sprawling farmstead called Wheysike House. After about half a mile you come to a stile in a wall, which you cross. Continue with a wall on your right and the beck on your left, until you come to **Saur Hill Bridge**. Climb the stone step stile to reach the bridge. There is a PW signpost here. **High Force** is 3¾ miles behind you; **Cauldron Snout** is 3½ miles to the left (across the bridge); and Langdon Beck youth hostel and East Underhurth Farm (B&B) are up the track on your right.

There is little accommodation in this area so it is worth booking it in advance if you can. The track to the right takes you to the B6277. The hostel is on the left (it is a T-shaped stone building, surrounded by hedges, with solar panels on one of the roofs). The hostel building dates back to 1965. A plaque in the common room has a phoenix with a Latin inscription beneath, 'ex cinere resurrexi', which roughly translates as 'risen from the ashes' and relates to the previous hostel, which stood on this spot. The former hostel had a central concrete section with two cedar annexes either side (one for males and one for females). In November 1958, just before it closed up for the winter, it burnt down. A possible cause was a gas ring, which was thought to have been left on when some hostellers went out for a walk. The farm B&B is up a track on its right. There is a public telephone box here. To the left, further up the road is the Langdon Beck Hotel built in 1887.

Section 12 – Langdon Beck to Dufton

Distance – 12.1 miles / 19.4 km
Height gained on PW route – 330 m (1,082 ft)
Height lost on PW route – 540 m (1,772 ft)

Route outline: Langdon Beck to Widdy Bank Farm; Cauldron Snout; Birkdale Farm; Moss Shop; Maize Beck; High Cup Nick; Dufton.

Birkdale

Section 12.1

Retrace your steps to **Saur Hill Bridge**. Cross the bridge and continue ahead towards the whitewashed farm buildings up ahead (**Sayer Hill Farm**). When you get there aim for a PW signpost, which directs you left, up the slope, (wire fence on your right) away from the farm. The path swings slightly right to a stone step stile in a wall ahead. There is a prominent tree to the left of the stile. You descend, down a grassy slope to a marshy area with three sets of duckboards to help keep your feet dry. Continue ahead to another stone step stile in another wall, then, crossing another section of duckboards, cross another stone step stile in a third wall. This one has a small sprung wooden gate on top. Here you descend to a second boggy area with planks (**South Loom Sike**). You then go up the slope to a fourth wall, which also has a stone stile with a sprung wooden gate on top and a metal farm gate on its left, with yet another 'Bull in field' sign (the field is certainly there but no sign of any bulls on my visits). Cross the stile. There is a bench ahead, if you need a stop.

When I passed the bench in 2012 it had a brass plaque on it with a dedication – 'Albert Cradock Gibson, 20-11-28 – 20-7-01 He loved this place'. In July 2013 when I passed it again, a second plaque has been added – 'Margery Gibson, 26-1-32 – 8-9-12, Hail to thee blithe spirit!' You are now on a bank, high above the Tees. The path between **Saur Hill Bridge** and the bench has cut across a corner of a triangle with **Langdon Beck** forming one side and the **River Tees** forming the other. The whitewashed buildings ahead are **Widdy Bank Farm.**

The PW descends down a bank to a wooden step stile in a wire fence and once again, with the **River Tees** on your left, goes ahead on the flat to a stone step stile, with a small sprung wooden gate on top, in the wall around the farm. The marker post here has a white acorn on top and a Durham County Council notice on it informing walkers 'This public right of way has been diverted by statutory order. Please follow waymarks' (this is a reminder that the PW is not a static footpath but is constantly changing). You leave the walled area via a second stone step stile with a wooden gate on top, next to the metal farm gate. With the farm away to your right, the path is very obvious. The path follows a wide green track. A grey coloured barn is passed, away to the right, and then you go through a wooden kissing gate in a wire fence, which crosses the path. After this, the path is right by the Tees and it narrows as the Tees curves around **Widdybank Fell** on your right. There are boulders underfoot in places and you need to be careful to avoid turning an ankle or going into the river. In other places there are duckboards and slabs to help you on your way. There are three areas on this section where ancient rock falls will slow your progress down a bit. You know the worst is behind you when you reach a large cairn close to the path on the right, followed by a long section of duckboards. The Tees arcs away to your left, whilst you walk between **Falcon Clints** above you on your right, and **Lingy Holm** on your left. The flagstones return for a while on a very beautiful section of the Tees. There is heather on either side of the path and in the summer sunshine it is a good place for a photograph.

After heavy rain the path can be quite wet underfoot. There are eels in the Tees here. I saw one close to the waters edge when I passed by in late July 2013 after twelve hours of overnight rain the night before.

The boulders in the path return after the slabs. Ahead on a hill, a stone barn can be seen. You pass this later on. Eventually the path curves round to the right and you begin your climb up the side of **Cauldron Snout**.

This is one of the highlights of the walk but very difficult to photograph. Fortunately many modern digital cameras now have video too, which captures it better. I am a strong supporter of digital cameras. When I first walked the PW in the 1970s I carried a 35mm camera, which held either 24 or 36 exposures (films or slides). I used it sparingly, both because of the expense, (of the film and the developing) and the fact that I usually only carried a few films and they were hard to replace during the walk. This was a shame as I missed out on taking quite a few early photos of the PW. Now even a standard 4Gb chip can easily hold well over 5,000 photos at 3Mb file size. My current camera has a 16Gb chip and I take photos at 8Mb. I can quite easily shoot off 1,700 pictures every time I walk the PW.

The climb beside **Cauldron Snout** is within the bounds of all but the unsteadiest walkers but again care should be exercised on this section of the route. The final plunge comes first. This is very exciting. Next follows a series of very small waterfalls as the Tees quickly tumbles down the hillside on a narrow groove of whin sill. The path scrambles up the hillside with the river on the left. Eventually, a grey stone dam appears on the skyline ahead. The path levels off when you can see a footbridge ahead, in front of the dam. You reach a tarmac road to the right of the bridge. Langdon Beck Hotel can be reached by going right on the road (but it is a long walk!). PW walkers are directed left by the PW signpost on the other side of the road. Next to it is a Natural England sign welcoming you to Moor House – Upper Teesdale National Nature Reserve.

> The bridge was built in 1966. Cow Green Reservoir was built, after a Parliamentary enquiry, between 1967 and 1971 for the Tees Valley and Cleveland Water Board in order to supply industries further down the river. It was vigorously opposed by conservationists who objected to the destruction of several species of rare alpine plants known to grow on the site. Many of these were moved to new locations before and during building work.

Section 12.2

Turn left on the tarmac road, and shortly afterwards, at a farm gate leading to **Birkdale** (about ½ mile away), turn left up the farm track, and over a cattle grid. A dry stone wall will be on your right. If you look back, near the first bend in the track, you should be able to see a bend in the Tees with the PW clearly visible on the ground next to it. Follow the **Birkdale** track, past a barn on your left, over a second cattle grid, past a second barn, over a third cattle grid, and past a third barn. This one has a name on the OS maps - **Dale Byre**. You next go through a wooden gate, over a sike, and shortly, at the PW signpost with a blue chevron (**Dufton** 8 mls), turn left down the track to **Birkdale Farm** (see photograph at beginning of this section).

This is quite an isolated place but in its heyday it was a staging post on an important drove road between the Southern Uplands in Scotland and Malham. It is no surprise that in 1948, Tom Stephenson chose the Tees and the route over to **Dufton** as part of his selling of the Pennine Way to a key group of MPs who accompanied him on the walk.

Go up the track, into the farmyard, (tree on the left and farm buildings on the right) and through a metal gate on the other side. Continue ahead on the track, through a second, wooden gate in the dry stone wall that crosses the track. There is a kissing gate on the left but the gate is easier if you are in a group. Before the farm track turns right, and before a metal gate across the track, continue ahead to a prominent footbridge over **Grain Beck**. There is also a PW signpost here. There are five stone steps up to the footbridge.

This is an indication of the potential variations in the water level of the streams around here as although the beck will probably be calm, Kettlegrain Sike, Foxyard Sike, Maingrain Sike, Thistlyhill Sike and Goldenmea Sike, plus several other sikes, which don't have names, all feed into it.

The Way now ascends the hillside ahead on a section of slabs to the right of an old miners' track which is soon joined, to **Moss Shop**, the site of an old lead mine. On the way up, you will probably see some red flags flying as there is a military firing range (**Warcop**) to the left of the path (I have been this way a dozen times and I have yet to hear any firing). The track goes up an old spoil heap, where there is one of these flags, next to a notice board. There are good views back towards **Birkdale Farm** and **Falcon Clints** from here. At the spoil heap the track veers to the right and then back to the left again. Flags appear alongside the path in places. The path ascends westerly and becomes faint in places as the way underfoot becomes grassy. You come to a wooden two-plank bridge, which you cross. Later the path crosses over **Stoneymea Sike** by means of a slab stone bridge. A cairn on the left of the path marks the end of the ups, and now is the time to head downhill to meet **Maize Beck**. Keep an eye open for a small wooden marker post with a yellow dot on it, as it is here that you veer slightly left to a two-plank bridge over **Horseman Sike**. There are several other wooden or slab bridges over ditches which you cross on your descent to **Maize Beck**. If the mist isn't about, you should have a clear view of **Maize Beck** away down the slope to the left and ahead. Follow the path, slabbed in places, until it reaches the bank above **Maize Beck**, where it descends on a parallel path to the waterside.

Section 12.3

The PW follows a green path, with **Maize Beck** on your left. Again there are slabs on one section. After about half a mile you will come across a substantial metal bridge, high above the beck. Again this is in recognition of the fact that the previous bridge was washed away; lives have been lost crossing the beck in the past when it was in spate. Cross the bridge. In the middle on the right is a brass plaque in memory of Ken Willson MBE, 1914 - 2003, a former President of the Pennine Way Association. There are eight steps down from the bridge to the level ground on the other side. This new bridge avoids the need to take the old flood route on the northern bank of **Maize Beck**, which takes longer. In dry weather, it is possible to walk across the beck with dry feet. You now go up a track, parallel with the beck, which is now on your right. Soon the stony track becomes grassy. There are a few stone markers with gold painted directional arrows on them beside the path, and some wooden posts with yellow circles on them between the beck and **High Cup Nick** to guide you. After a while the track leaves the beck behind and goes roughly SW. The path eventually levels out as you approach **High Cup Plain**. Keep an eye open here for a small herd of semi-wild black horses that may be grazing near the path. There is little indication at this point on the route that you are about to see one of the highlights of the walk - **High Cup Nick**. You pass a fallen stone post on your left. Ahead you can see the hillside sloping down from both the left and the right, with level ground in the middle. You pass two more stone posts. When you reach a third, you begin your descent to **High Cup Nick** on your right. The 'nick' is a U-shaped gap at the edge of the plain where **High Cup Gill** flows over the edge into the spectacular glacial valley, which is **High Cup**.

On a clear sunny day, it is easy to take numerous photographs and to sit and take in its spectacular view. After heavy rain, several mountain streams gush spectacularly down the hillside into High Cupgill Beck, particularly **Strands Beck**, which goes from a trickle to fast flowing water, promising wet boots if you are not careful (see photograph at centre of book).

Section 12.4

Leave **High Cup Plain** by walking West, crossing **High Cup Gill**, and around the rim of the amphitheatre of **High Cup Nick**, following a faint path. At the edges of the plain, after walking up a slope, look out for a stone marker, where you should turn left. If you miss the marker, you need to turn left along the rim edge so that **High Cup** is on your left. A distinct path will appear as you initially ascend up the slope, and then descend. Two small streams cross the path and flow into **High Cup Gill**. One of these is **Strands Beck.** You are now on **Narrow Gate** (path), which gradually descends, and the occasional cairn appears by the path side. The path eventually swings into a small green valley, which is an old quarry. Above, on the hillside is an old limekiln. The last one you saw was by **God's Bridge** on the way into **Baldersdale**. You go through a metal gate in a wall ahead, and walk half right to another metal gate in a wall on the other side of the field. Descend to a metal farm gate with a kissing gate next to it. Go through the gate and descend along a track with a wall on your right. You soon come to another metal farm gate with a kissing gate next to it and enter a walled lane. The conical hill on the right is Dufton Pike.

The track descends past **Dod Hill**, on the right, past a stone barn, also on the right. Just before you reach the barn a track goes down on the left towards Keisley, with a stone barn further along it in the distance on the right (this view makes a nice photograph on a sunny day). There is a PW signpost here informing you that **High Cup Nick** is now 2¾ miles behind you. Ahead is **Dufton**. At the end of the walled track is a gate, which you go through. Ahead is a tarmac road. You descend on the road, pass **Bow Hall Farm** on the right, to meet a T-junction. Here is another PW signpost (**High Cup Nick** 3½ mls; **Dufton** ½ ml to the right). Here you leave the bridleway (blue chevron) and turn right on the road where the PW is technically a footpath as the finger post has a yellow chevron.

When the road bends sharp left, there is another PW signpost indicating that the pub, toilets, village shop and youth hostel are ahead on the road, but that PW walkers are now invited to turn right up a track, where **Garrigill** is 15 miles away.

> This section of the PW doesn't go through the village and has little value as all the accommodation can be reached by following the road. If you are a purist, return to this point tomorrow. I have done this section around Dufton on a warm day and it is much nicer along the road (honest!); less flies and no overgrown vegetation.

If you are a purist, you will need to go up the stony lane for a couple of hundred yards until you get to five-bar wooden fence on your left. Look for a three-finger PW signpost here, directing you left (Pennine Way with a yellow chevron) through a small wooden gate, along a narrow sunken slabbed path beside a small wet ditch (loads of flies in hot weather). The path then goes between two wire fences. You next cross two wooden gates quite close together. Later, still on an enclosed path, you cross a bend in **Eller Beck** by means of two stone clapper bridges (one quite ancient and the other a slabbed bridge) and continue ahead, again on a narrow enclosed path between two wire fences (topped with barbed wire so be careful here) which changes to a wall on one side and trees on another, to meet a PW signpost on the farm track to **Coatsike Farm**.

If you need to go back into **Dufton** for your overnight accommodation, turn left here, down the track, and return to this point tomorrow.

The village of **Dufton** was originally built by the Anglo Saxons and the name means settlement of the doves. On the way through the village you pass, on the left, Grandie Caravan Park (which takes tents), a public phone box, the village toilets and the youth hostel. On the right is the village green with a red painted drinking fountain, which I have always admired. With the Cumbrian red sandstone houses and Dufton Pike in the background, it is always worth a picture or two on your camera. There is a Latin inscription around the top of the fountain ("*Fons est inlimis, nitidis argenteus undis Quem necque pastores nec pastae monte capellae Inficiunt. Aliudve pecus: quem nulla volucris Nec fera perturbat: nec lapsus ab arbore ramus*") which J.H.B. Peel, in his book '*Along the Pennine Way*', (1979, p119) describes as 'a watery pun of poor Latin'. It was placed there in 1858 by a Mr Wallace of the London Lead Company and roughly translated says: "*There is a clear pool, whose waters gleam like silver. It is not tainted by shepherds, or by their she-goats grazing on the mountain. Nor is it muddied by cattle, or by birds or wild animals, or by a branch fallen from a tree*" (for further information see http://www.duftonvillage.info/page16.html).

Across the green is the Stag Inn, with the conical shaped Dufton Pike in the distance behind it. If you are lucky, you can also see the white 'golf ball' on top of **Great Dun Fell**, which is left of Dufton Pike. This is a radar station, used by air traffic control, and you will pass this on your way to **Alston** tomorrow.

Section 13 - Dufton to Alston

Distance – 19.4 miles / 31.5 km
Height gained on PW route – 1,010 m (3,314 ft)
Height lost on PW route – 1,030 m (3,379 ft)

Route outline: Dufton to Coatsike Farm; Halsteads; Knock Old Man; Dunfell Hush; Great Dun Fell; Little Dun Fell; Cross Fell; Greg's Hut; Longman Hill; Garrigill; South Tyne Bridge; Bleagate; Alston.

Knock Old Man (Currick) – the 'original' form of signage

If you haven't taken the official PW route out of **Dufton**, and you feel that you absolutely must, you need to walk about 200 yards back along the road (from the youth hostel). The route description is given at the end of section 12. If you haven't, and you feel that your longest day on the PW so far (19.4 miles), coupled with 1,010 metres (3,314 feet) of ascent, and the fact that all the height you lost yesterday needs to be regained, and more, is enough for one day's walk, read on.

Warning! This is one of the longest days without too many features or signage to aid navigation, and there are some parts where the line of the PW on the ground can be very faint (this is despite the passage of feet over several decades). If you are walking without a GPS, then it would be advisable to prepare your compass bearings for the more featureless sections of terrain (for example for about a kilometre after **Knock Old Man** and traversing the summit plateau of **Cross Fell**), which could be vital if visibility is poor.

Section 13.1

From the village green, continue ahead (NW) along the tarmac road, past Dufton youth hostel on the left. Keep on the road as it bends right, and goes past **Hall Croft** B&B on the left, and the road to Long Marton. Further up, the road bends to the left towards Knock and Coney Garth B&B, but you continue ahead, on a lane, which leads to a farm track to **Coatsike Farm**. The signpost here says Public Footpath, rather than the expected Pennine Way but that is because, as you know, the official PW cuts around the village and joins the farm track further ahead. You will pass the PW signpost on the right as you go up the track. Go up the lane, crossing **Eller Beck**, bearing left at a PW signpost, past a bungalow on the left and then northwards, along a narrow gravel track to go through two gates, one before, and one after **Coatsike Farm**, which is passed on the right.

A third gate, with a wooden step stile next to it on the right, takes you onto a sunken tree-lined lane, called **Hurning Lane**. Passing through several gaps, two stiles and three wooden gates (two new), you ascend along the enclosed track to the ruined farmstead of **Halsteads**, passed on the left. Go through a metal gate by the farmstead and continue on the track, passing a newly created artificial pond on your left. The track soon descends right, around **Cosca Hill**, with a wire fence on the left, to a metal gate in a wall. Go through the gate, or the narrow stone step stile next to it. The stream on the other side of the gate is **Great Rundale Beck**, which has a very photogenic stone clapper bridge over it, which you cross. Keep ahead on the track to a wall, where the track bears half right to follow it (wall on your left). The track goes in a straight line up the hillside. At first there is a wall on the left and open countryside on the right. A wall then appears on the right and for several yards you are in a walled lane. When the wall on the left disappears go through a kissing gate, next to a wooden gate. The wall on the right continues for a short distance. At another kissing gate, next to a metal gate, you join a green track and this soon bears left, away from the wall, to cross a small burn, called, surprisingly, **Small Burn**! The green track now takes a shallow left curve up the hillside, and when the track bends right, at a PW signpost, continue ahead on a fairly level path, which soon descends, to a wire fence on the left, with a very rock strewn stream away to the left. You next reach and walk beside a dry stone wall on your left for a short distance. In good visibility, you should be able to see the path climbing up the hillside ahead on the left of the stream (**Swindale Beck**). Cross the wall using the stone steps built into the wall, to a second wall with a stone step stile. Note the yellow notice about the danger of old shafts and mine workings attached to the wooden fence around the stile.

Section 13.2

Ahead is a substantial metal footbridge over **Swindale Beck**, wide enough to take a small moon buggy that farmers use on the hills. There are a couple of piles of spare slabs in the green area beyond the bridge. Ignore the ladder stile over the wall on the left, which you pass. The PW bears right, with **Swindale Beck** on your right, along a narrow path. Go up a stepped section of the path to the Moor House Reserve sign between two posts. To the left of it is a stone marker with a yellow arrow indicating that you should continue up the hillside.

If you are lucky, in clear conditions you should be able to follow the narrow grassy path without difficulty. However, if the mist is down and it is raining, you will need to be very careful not to lose the path. The occasional cairn, stone marker and post will help. From the bridge you are essentially heading NE up the slope above the beck on your right. At the top of the slope ahead, the gradient becomes easier. The path goes left up beside **Knock Hush**, then right again to meet **Knock Old Man**.

Keep a sharp lookout on the ground for the path, which can be indistinct in places. Near the top of the slope you pass a stone marker, then two very distinctive cairns on the left close to the path. Between them is a view of the 'golf ball' on top of **Great Dun Fell** (in good weather). **Knock Hush** is quite distinctive (on the right of the path) as it is grassy and V-shaped. The PW follows a grassy path on the bank above it. Stone markers with gold painted arrows by the path help in navigation. Continue the gradual ascent, on the bank, high above the V-shaped hush on the right. Eventually, at one of the stone markers with a gold painted directional marker pointing ahead, the distinctive cairn near the summit of **Knock Fell** comes into view and the path takes you to it. This cairn or currick is called **Knock Old Man** on the OS map, and it is over six feet tall and essentially box-shaped with a pyramid of stones on the top (see photograph at the beginning of this section).

Again if you are lucky, and the weather is clear, navigation will not be a problem. From **Knock Old Man** you should be able to see a small cairn in the distance. The path between here and the tarmac road, (which goes from Knock to the summit of **Great Dun Fell**), is extremely faint in places and in poor weather it can be very easy to get misplaced. Remember that the road, unseen for quite a while yet, is away on your left (about half a mile). If you do get lost, and you have little chance of finding the path again, it is better to veer left to find the road and use this to get to the summit of **Great Dun Fell**.

The triangular cairn, (in the distance), after **Knock Old Man**, marks the summit of **Knock Fell** and you head for this on a narrow path through moorland grass. In mist you will probably need to follow a compass bearing so come prepared! After the cairn, the PW heads approximately NNW on very level ground, which descends ever so slightly. It is very difficult to follow in mist because of the stony ground which leaves no trace of the path, however, once you reach a slabbed section, the path becomes easy to follow. As I have said earlier, I am not a great lover of slabs but here they are most welcome! In sunnier weather, you will be able to see the radar station on top of **Great Dun Fell** so you can use this as a guide. Metal snow poles appear to the right of the path. These predate the slabs. The slabbed path descends down the slope and goes past a small tarn on the right, and passes a field study enclosure on the left. The slabs disappear and you continue down the grassy slope, with the snow poles on your right to guide you, and you finally reach the tarmac road (from Knock to the radar station on the top of **Great Dun Fell**) at a PW signpost. One finger post with a yellow chevron says **Dufton** and points back the way you have just walked. The second finger post, with a blue chevron says **Garrigill** and points right, up the tarmac road, towards **Great Dun Fell**.

> If you have been very unfortunate with the weather and have walked this far in almost zero visibility, and driving rain, the route finding is less complex from here. I have done this section almost a dozen times and I have been unfortunate with the weather for the majority of my walks. I hope you have more clement weather than I usually have.

Section 13.3

Turn right up the road for a short distance until you come to a second PW signpost, with three finger posts, by a wooden gate. One tells you that you are now 5½ miles from **Dufton**. A second is for the Pennine Way, and the third is for a bridleway which goes off to the right.

There is a metal object that looks a bit like a boot scraper here. If the weather is really bad and you can't see the path in front of you, a safer option is to follow the road all the way up to the summit.

Leave the road at the signpost and head NW on a peaty path. Directly across the path ahead is **Dunfell Hush**. The path reaches this then turns left along the top of it before descending into it via some steps, and then slabs climbing out the other side. Continuing in the same direction on a faint grass path, you should reach the fence around the radar station on the summit of **Great Dun Fell**.

Don't forget that the road is on your left during this section, so if the worst comes to the worst, head left toward it. The radar station resembles a prefabricated warehouse with added features; these look like a golf ball with a couple of button mushrooms plus some antennae. You will see what I mean when you see them in the flesh.

Turn right here and follow the fence. You will come to some slabs, which you follow into a dip and then up a grassy slope to reach **Little Dun Fell**.

If the weather is bad, there is a basic wind shelter here where you can catch your breath and take on some food to keep you going. I can't emphasise enough how important good waterproofs are on the PW. The crossing of this section in bad weather will test them to their absolute limit!

After **Little Dun Fell** you descend to a col known as **Crowdundle Head**.

Crowdundle Head is a watershed. On the right is Tees Head, the collecting point for the **River Tees**. The water collected on the ground to your left, will eventually flow into the Irish Sea.

As you descend, you pick up the slabs once again. There is an old fence, which used to have a stile here, but now the slabbed path goes between the wooden posts. The fence is an old boundary fence between the old counties of Cumberland and Westmorland. You now climb up the last bit, which takes you to the summit plateau of **Cross Fell**. This summit is really flat so in bad weather you need to have your wits about you. The entrance cairn is very tall and thin, and sited within a rock strewn area. You go slightly west of NW on a grassy path towards a bell-shaped cairn. When you reach that, continue in the same direction towards a large cross-shelter made out of stones. Near it is a trig point (S 2979). The cross-shelter is a bit like the one you saw on **Shunner Fell** only several times larger, but unfortunately in 2013, it was in a poor state of repair.

> You are now over half way across the summit plateau, and have reached a height of 893 metres (2,930 feet), which is the highest point on the Pennine Way. **The Cheviot** summit is only 815 metres (2,676 feet). **Cross Fell** seems to have its own microclimate sometimes. It certainly has its own wind, called the Helm Wind, which can localise the weather around it.

Again, it is worth preparing a compass bearing beforehand to help you with navigation from the shelter to the exit cairn on **Cross Fell**. Leave roughly NNW towards a triangular-shaped cairn, and then descend to a large bell-shaped cairn at the exit point. Its top section has been repaired several times, but you can still see the craftsmanship that went into it. Its shape is really an acorn which reflects the acorn sign for a National Trail. If the weather is bad, you will need to rely on map and compass. You descend down the (initially) grassy north flank of the summit, through a rocky area (where **Crossfell Well** is) then back to grass, on quite a narrow path, to meet a track at a cairn, crossing from left to right.

This is the old corpse road from **Garrigill** to Kirkland, so named because at one time, **Garrigill** had no consecrated ground and so the dead had to be taken to Kirkland for burial. In extreme weather, the coffins had to be abandoned and collected when the weather became kinder!

Section 13.4

Turn right on the track. There is a new wire fence away to your left as you descend down the track. The fence comes to meet the PW, and when you reach the fence corner, you go through a wooden gate across the track. In about half a mile ahead, along the track, you will reach a mountain refuge hut called **Greg's Hut**.

Greg's Hut is maintained by the Mountain Bothies Association who have saved many a walker's life through their dedicated volunteers. If you use any of their huts, consider a small donation or even membership, or maybe join one of their working parties. It a good place to take a rest and drink some coffee if you are carrying a small lightweight flask. If the weather on the tops has been bad, you will hopefully be under it here. From **Greg's Hut**, it is reasonably straightforward to **Garrigill** and you have a good track all the way down. You should be able to see the track contour around the hillside ahead (it bends to the left around it). The track can be a bit hard underfoot but there is a grass verge in most places which you can use to take some of the pounding off your feet. The estate has done quite a lot of work on the track recently so that in 2013, when I last walked it, the track was in extremely good repair.

After about 10 minutes you pass some old mine workings on your right, below a stream. The whole area is riddled with old mine shafts and levels. Shortly after a second set of old mine workings you come across the first stone PW marker for quite a while. The PW is straight ahead on the track. The marker has an arrow to the right and an 'Ω' (this is really a horseshoe as it is a bridleway).

In this area, you will see small purple stones in the track, particularly if it is wet underfoot. These are fluorspar, which is used in steel making. I sometimes collect a few of the darker purple coloured ones to take home as a souvenir.

Soon after the stone marker you pass through a wooden gate in a fence. The track continues its gradual descent towards **Garrigill**. You pass a track on the left which heads towards some disused mines near Cash Burn and Bullman Sike. Shortly after, you pass a track on the right, which leads to more abandoned mining activity on **Long Man Hill**. The main track ascends slightly to **Pikeman Hill** where the fence comes close to the track (don't forget to look back here as you can see the summit of **Great Dun Fell** along this section, and on a clear day, you can see **Greg's Hut** from here too!). You go through a metal gate in the fence and start descending towards a walled lane.

There is a sign on one of the gate posts about rodent traps, and if you look into the ditch alongside the track you will occasionally see a narrow log spanning the ditch with a cage on top (to protect the birds), and a sprung trap in the centre.

The track is well maintained here. Just before you enter a walled lane there is a PW signpost (no mileage) near a pool on your left. Soon after, you go through a metal gate across the track. There is a second (new) signpost with three finger posts, where the walled lane bends sharply to the right. Two finger posts relate to the PW and the third points to a footpath to Leadgate directly ahead. You should be able to see the village of **Garrigill** ahead as you descended the final hill. Before you come to the end of the walled lane there is a third (new) signpost with two finger posts and at the bottom of the lane, where it meets the tarmac road, there is another one with blue chevrons (**Garrigill** ½ mile, **Dufton** 15 miles). Better late than never I suppose. The last one is for the benefit of walkers heading south.

Section 13.5

At the tarmac road, you now share the PW with the **South Tyne Trail** for several miles. Turn left and walk into the centre of the village. There is a post office and shop here (which has a King George VI letter box in the wall) that does B&B. Also facing the village green is the **George and Dragon Inn**, which alas was closed in late 2013 (hopefully new tenants will be found for it soon). After a hard crossing of the tops, you may well need a break here and there is a nice shady tree with seats around it opposite the post office. This makes a good place for a boots-off break. Ignore the road to **Alston**, and continue ahead on the tarmac road past the old school house, (a large white painted pebble dashed building with a terracotta coloured plaque set into the building's wall), where the road bends to the left. Keep an eye open for a PW signpost on the right by a gate (**Alston** 3¾ miles). Go through the gate, down a cinder track, past a large spoil heap on the right, to a second signpost by a wire fence on the left. Walk ahead in the direction of the finger post, along the wire fence, to a stone step stile in a stone wall, with an old metal garden gate in front, which you cross. A nice green path takes you up the slope to a second stone stile with a short guidepost on the left. After you cross it you descend down the slope on an obvious grassy path towards a wall corner ahead, passing a small guidepost, to reach a path along the riverside (**River South Tyne**) with the river on your right and a wall on your left (either close by, or next to the path). Keep to the riverside path, which soon becomes tree-lined, crossing several stiles. The last stile is quite interesting as it is a wooden step over stile with a V- shaped gap in the top. Here there is a line of tape on the right which you follow to a green metal footbridge over the river, with stone steps leading up to it. There is a PW signpost just before it. Cross over the bridge.

Continue in the same direction as before with the **River South Tyne** now on your left. After a short distance on a wide path, look out for a PW signpost on the right which directs you up a narrow path, up the bank, away from the river. Go over the stone step stile in the wall ahead and continue uphill to a prominent three-pointer PW signpost on the skyline, next to a stone bench. Continue ahead to a gateway (keep an eye out for a bull that may be in the field here), passing a farm on the right as you do (**Low Sillyhall**). Ahead through a wooden gate then a gap in a field wall. There are marker posts with yellow directional arrows on them to guide you here. Go through a wooden gate, past a building (barn) on the left to a stone step stile in the wall. The build-ings ahead on the right are **Bleagate Farm**. Pass the farm, go over another stone step stile, through two openings in the walls ahead to another stile, passing a barn on the right, then a house on the right, to another stone step stile. Now you go round an old wooded quarry on your right, over two stone step stiles, through two gaps in walls to descend to a footbridge (over **Nattrass Gill**) on the left. There is a PW signpost on the other side of the footbridge. Continue ahead over two more stone step stiles, a kissing gate, and a gap to eventually reach a gate at the entrance to a narrow lane. There is a PW signpost here. This is popular with local dog walkers so take care underfoot! The lane will take you into **Alston**. The grey painted building up the bank on the right, before you reach the market town, is **Alston** youth hostel. There is a new (2013) PW signpost here. **Garrigill**, along the PW and **South Tyne Trail** is 3¾ miles behind you. The **South Tyne Trail** continues ahead on the track. The PW goes down the slope to a stone step stile and the road where there is another PW signpost. If you have booked into the youth hostel, there are some stone steps up to it from the Pennine Way. This is a purpose built PW hostel opened on 11 October 1975.

Alston is a great place for a rest after the hard walk over from **Dufton**. It has plenty of shops, two banks, a chippie, bakery, Co-op, chemist etc. There is also a brand new Spar (2012) on the left side of the **A686** (on the way into the town) where they sell basic foodstuffs. The youth hostel is affiliated to the YHA and has very friendly people there. It is my first choice when I look for accommodation here.

Alston has a narrow gauge railway as unfortunately British Railways closed the branch line to Haltwhistle on 1 May 1976. The good news is that the South Tynedale Railway runs steam trains from **Alston** to **Kirkhaugh** on several days of the week (check their website for full details of train times). The South Tyne Trail runs alongside the railway line as far as **Kirkhaugh** and then continues to Lambley Viaduct where you can cut across to the road to rejoin the PW. It would make a nice circular walk if you want one. There is also a very photographic signal box at the railway station in **Alston**. Have a look around the town too. A house next to the Angel Inn dates back to 1681. It is a great place to take a day off and to catch up on shopping and washing.

Section 14 - Alston to Greenhead

Distance – 16.5 miles / 26.5 km
Height gained on PW route – 545 m (1,788 ft)
Height lost on PW route – 675 m (2,214 ft)

Route outline: Alston to Harbut Lodge; Gilderdale Burn; Whitley Castle; Kirkhaugh Farm; Lintley Farm; Slaggyford; Burnstones; Glendue Burn; Maiden Way; A689; Hartley Burn; Batey Shield; Greenriggs; Black Hill; A69; Greenhead.

View from A689 towards Black Burn and Holly Rigg

Section 14.1

At the youth hostel, by the PW signpost, go down the slope, through the trees to cross a stone step stile in a low wall next to the road (**A686**) and turn left along the road and cross the road bridge over the **River South Tyne**. Fork right at the war memorial onto the **A689** then, at a PW signpost with a yellow chevron (**Slaggyford** 5¼ miles) turn right and descend down a lane which is the driveway to a cottage further up. Go through a metal gate across the drive to the cottage (**Grey Hounds**) and take the small wooden gate to the left of the house into a passageway with a wooden fence on one side and a dry stone wall with trees on the other. After the house boundary fence is passed, a field fence, then a hedge, replaces it and the narrow path takes you to a stone step stile and sprung wooden gate. After you cross the stile, a wall is now on your right and an open field on your left. Continue ahead and cross a track ahead, go through a wooden gate (or use the kissing gate next to it), under some power lines, through a gap in a wall ahead, then along a grassy track to the old **Harbut Lodge** gates. There are small wooden gates either side of the ornate wooden gate. Go through the old lodge gates, through a short tree-lined track for a few yards which takes you over **Eller Well**, past a guidepost on your right. The PW then takes you round a small field, with a wire fence on your left, past what looks like a shed, where you turn left, through a metal gate. Go ahead with a dry stone wall on your left and a house on your right. Turn right to pass in front of the house. The house has a small gravel garden in front with a three-bar wooden fence covered with wire (possibly against rabbits), and if you look on the stonework to the right of the door (without staring), you can see a faded (painted) PW and arrow (dating back to the 1970s). Finally, you follow the field edge, which curves around in an arc (anticlockwise) until you reach a stone step stile in the wall next to a PW signpost. When I used it in late July 2013 there was a home-made wooden gate made up of pallets across the entrance to the stile. Cross the stile and turn left along the track back to the road (**A689**). Turn right along the road for a short distance to a PW signpost (**Alston** 1 mile and **Slaggyford** 4½ miles) on the opposite side of the road.

Cross over the road (with care) and go through the wooden kissing gate (white acorn on the left post) to the right of a metal farm gate. The farm ahead is **Harbut Law**. The PW here shares the path with Isaac's Tea Trail. Go ahead, through a second metal gate in the stone wall to the right of the farm buildings. Ahead up the slope, across a stream (**Wanwood Well**), initially with a stone wall on your left, but the path drifts half right to go over a stone step stile in the stone wall ahead. Walk ahead across rough pasture through a kissing gate in a wall (next to a wooden gate), through a second kissing gate (next to a metal gate), then a metal gate to descend to a stone step stile with a sprung wooden gate and a footbridge over **Gilderdale Burn**. Cross the footbridge and the wooden step stile at the end of it. You now climb out of the dip, with a stone wall on your right, to a kissing gate, next to a metal gate. Go through this and continue uphill (fence on your left) to a second kissing gate (and metal gate). Continue ahead to meet a track, which takes you to a metal gate in a fence.

Look to your right to see the earthen foundations of a Roman Auxiliary Fort on the Maiden Way called **Whitley Castle**. The **Maiden Way** is a Roman Road, which ran between Bravoniacum, near Kirkby Thorne, and Carvoran near **Greenhead**. There is not much to see there now but you can still make out the ditches and earth banks (ramparts), which made up defences of the fort. There are four ramparts on the southern three sides and incredibly, seven on the northern side. It is more impressive if you go online and look at an aerial photograph of it.

The track curves around to the left of the fort, and you head for a ladder stile in the wall on your right. There is a metal gate next to it. This takes you down the slope (stream on your left) to a kissing gate. You cross the stream via a footbridge and continue downhill, through a small wood, to the road (stream now away on your right) which you reach via a stone step stile. There is a PW signpost with a yellow chevron on the finger post pointing back the way you have just come (**Alston** 3 miles).

Diagonally, over the road (cross with care), on the left, is another PW signpost with a yellow chevron (**Slaggyford** 2½ miles). Go through the metal gate and bear left across the field to a wooden gate, then a wooden kissing gate in the four-bar wooden fence on your right, just before **Dyke House** (farm). There is a PW signpost here too. Pass the farm on your left (wall on your left by the farm), passing through three wooden gates, then a metal gate before descending to a farm track at **Kirkhaugh** (farm). There is a PW signpost here directing you to turn left on the track (down the track on the right is a stone bridge over the railway line). Turn left up the track, past the farm, to a PW signpost by a wooden gate on the right. Go over the cattle grid next to it.

The PW now skirts around a slope and pasture land with the **A689** on your left and the South Tyne Trail on the right (which is along-side the narrow gauge railway run by the South Tynedale Railway Preservation Society which runs from the old British Rail station in **Alston** to Lintley Halt). You cross two ladder stiles over stone walls, go through a wooden gate in a fence, then three more ladder stiles over stone walls, to reach a track which runs from the **A689** to **Lintley Farm** (which is under the railway bridge on your right). Here you cross the track and continue ahead to go through some trees, over a foot-bridge over **Thornhope Burn**, under **Lintley Viaduct**, to a wooden kissing gate at the edge of the trees. Continue on a path with the burn on your right, as it curves around a field to the left, then you go through a gate (white acorn on the right post).

The next short section is quite interesting as during the summer months, a flat walk between two kissing gates involves walking through chest high (I am over six feet tall) vegetation. After this there follows, (depending on the weather), a sometimes muddy and rocky path along the **River South Tyne** on your right. Tree roots may trip you along this section so be careful where you put your feet! You go through a number of gates, to reach a concrete road bridge (**Thompson's Well Bridge**). There is a PW signpost here (**Alston** 5¾ and **Slaggyford** ½ - there are no 'miles' on this signpost). Here you rejoin the road (**A689**) and continue ahead on the road into **Slaggyford** itself. 'Slaggy' comes from the Middle English 'slag', meaning slippery with mud. You might have experienced some of this on your walk along the river.

Section 14.2

At the fork in the road in the village, turn left, up the minor road, to **Yew Tree Chapel** on the right. Here, you need to turn right and pass in front of the chapel. To the left of the chapel, almost hidden in the shrubbery is a PW signpost with a yellow chevron which announces that **Burnstones** is 1½ miles away.

If you have the time, walk a little way up the road where you will see the 90 yard platform of the old Slaggyford railway station with its old green and white painted wooden railway station. This was built in 1890, and housed the booking office and two waiting rooms. The old Station Master's house, on the other side of the tracks is now a private residence. It is well worth going there as it is very photogenic. At the railway station the old railway track is the South Tyne Trail, which runs first to the left of the Pennine Way, then, after **Knar Burn**, to the right, as far as **Burnstones**, where the Pennine Way climbs out of the valley. It is quite useful if you want to do a circular walk. **Slaggyford** is five miles from **Alston** via the Trail, and it is another four miles to the Lambley Viaduct. If you chose to do a circular walk using the South Tyne Trail there are few exit points due to the embankments. The best walk is along the trail as far as Bowden's Bank where there is access to the **A689** and you could reconnect with the PW at the stile (shown in the picture at the start of this section),

Passing **Yew Tree Chapel** on your left go along a lane, going through two metal gates and crossing a footbridge, then a second footbridge over **Knar Burn**, before coming to a railway bridge on the left with a wooden gate in front of it. Turn left here and go through the wooden gate (white acorn marker on the gate), and under the railway bridge, through a second wooden gate on the other side of the bridge, up a grassy bank, (stone marker with PW carved into it here) with a wire fence on your left, then half right to a metal gate in a stone wall. Go through this then ahead on a track to a metal gate in a wire fence in front of a farm (**Merry Knowe**). There is a PW signpost here. Go through the gate and turn right, with the buildings on your left, and a wire fence on your right, to a stone stile by the side of a barn. Cross this, and two more stone step stiles passing several more buildings. In front of the third stile is a stone PW marker directing you half right towards a gate in a wall. Continue in the same direction over rough pasture (the old railway line (South Tyne Trail) is on your right). The white painted building ahead is **Knarsdale Hall** (shown as **Burnstones** on the OS map and PW signposts). Cross a ladder stile in the wall ahead, then a stone step stile before descending down a bank to a little two-plank bridge with a hand rail on its left. This replaced a similar bridge that was sited a few yards away. You can still see the slab foundations sticking out of the bank. Use this to cross **Coal Sike** and continue ahead through rough pasture to a wooden gate up ahead, and over a tarmac road. There is a PW signpost with a yellow chevron on one side of the road, pointing back (**Slaggyford** 1¼) and another one on the other side of the road, pointing forward (**Burnstones** ¼).

Cross the stile and continue ahead to a ladder stile in the wall ahead, then onto a wooden step stile (next to a wooden gate) in a wire fence, then ahead in the same direction to a small five-bar wooden gate in a stone wall ahead. The impressive building ahead on the left, across **Thinhope Burn**, is **Knarsdale Hall (Burnstones)**. Go through the gate and down some grassy steps in the slope and along a grassy path with a stone wall on the left. At the end of the wall is a stone hut. Immediately in front of it is the impressive **Burnstones** viaduct. To the right of the hut is a small wooden gate which you go through and you pass under one of the arches of the viaduct and through a metal gate to reach the road (**A689**).

Section 14.3

Turn left on the road and go under the viaduct again, this time on the road. By the driveway to the hall is a gate and a PW signpost directing you to a kissing gate not far ahead. You cross a wooden footbridge, and then you continue up the slope to a second kissing gate set in the dry stone wall ahead. You now bear right onto a track, which is the course of an old Roman Road (**Maiden Way**).

> This section over the rough pasture is relatively new (created in 2009) diverting the path away from **Burnstones**.

Go through a wooden gate across the track, and then just before the track bends left, where the wall is now on the right of the track, there is a PW signpost directing you onto a grassy path through the reeds on the right. You keep the wall to your right as you contour around **Proudy Hill**, before descending to **Glendue Burn**. On the way, you cross a wooden ladder stile (acorn on the right upright) to the right of a wooden gate, pass a barn on your right, cross **Proudyhill Sike**, go through a metal gate (with a wooden step stile next to it), over a small ladder stile over a wire fence then almost immediately after, over a wooden single step stile (wooden grab post on the left) over a second wire fence. You then descend on a grassy track to another wooden step stile before bending left, across a section of slabs, to a wooden footbridge over **Glendue Burn**. There are a lot of ferns and marsh grass here. Not a good place to linger except in sunny weather, and even then you might get midges.

Cross a wooden step stile in the fence ahead and ascend up the bank to a stone step stile in a stone wall, which you cross (one of the steps was broken in late July 2013). The wall is now on your left, and again, you are following in the footsteps of the Romans as you are once again on the **Maiden Way**. Unfortunately you won't see either a maiden or Roman today. Instead you ascend a slope, crossing a wooden step stile, with a wooden grab post, in a fence which crosses the path. A short while later, you cross another wooden step stile but this one has a huge wooden platform resting on railway sleepers on either side of the stile. I can only think that it is used by grouse shooters as a resting place so it might be removed when you pass by!

A fence replaces the wall, and you cross a wooden step stile in a fence ahead, then you pass a wooden step stile on your left (don't cross the fence, keep it on the left). Continue ahead through the rushes to a second wooden step stile with wooden platforms ahead. You pass a second wooden step stile on your left. The path now descends towards the **A689** road (ahead) again. You next come to a refurbished wooden step stile in the fence on your left with a new (2013) wooden grab post with a white acorn on it. The grab post was very bendy when I used it so it might be broken by the time you get to it. There is an unhelpful yellow directional arrow on the wooden upright above the stile. This time you must cross over the stile and go ahead towards a stone marker with 'PW' carved (and painted white) into it. Continue in the same direction on an indistinct path, with occasional white marker posts which will hopefully take you down the slope on the right to meet the road at a wooden step stile over a wire fence with a PW signpost. The route is really quite difficult to follow on the ground between the step stile and the road so be careful on this section.

Section 14.4

There is a ladder stile and PW signpost (see photograph at the beginning of this section) on the opposite side of the **A689** road which has been your constant companion on and off since you left **Alston**. The signpost pointing back says '**Burnstones** 3'. The one over the road says 'Pennine Way Public Footpath'. The top of the ladder stile is almost at road height and you leave the **A689** for the last time and descend the stile to the path below. You then descend the slope with the stone wall on your left, towards a ruined building with a tree next to it, which is on the other side of the wall (the middle section of the grey slate roof is missing). You pass the partial ruin, and when the wall bends to the left, continue ahead in the same direction. Slabs take you over **Black Burn**. More slabs guide you to a grassy mound with a stone PW marker on the top. This has a white painted acorn and a white arrow pointing half right. Go in that direction through rough pasture to a wooden step stile in a wire fence, almost hidden in the marsh grass. The cricket bat-like grab post has a white acorn on it. There is also an ancient PW signpost here, (which may have been replaced by the time you walk the route), which is moss covered.

You next pass through gaps in three low banks which have short posts with yellow directional markers on them. The grassy path then curves around a dip to climb up to a substantial rectangular shaped ruined stone building called **High House**. This used to be a barn, so the name is both confusing and puzzling. You now descend right, (keeping high initially) past some trees to a substantial (new) wooden footbridge over **Hartley Burn**, which replaced an old metal one.

Cross the burn via the footbridge, go through a small wooden gate at the end of the bridge, and turn left (PW directional post with acorn and yellow arrow), along the edge of the field, where there is a wire fence and the burn on your left. Cross a wooden step stile in a five-bar wooden gate, and climb up the bank through the trees, past a PW directional marker post, with acorn, to reach a wire fence. Continue ahead with the fence on your left, passing a wooden step stile in the fence with 'Not the Pennine Way' on the horizontal wooden bar on the top of the stile. This used to be the PW but it was amended many years ago. Do not cross it but continue up the slope to reach a wooden gate in a stone wall. There is a PW guidepost here.

Ahead, in the distance, is **Ulpham Farm** which has distinctive red painted doors. You will pass this on your way to **Kellah Burn** ahead. Behind, in the distance you can still see **High House.**

Go slightly left to pick up the fence on your left (guidepost) and descend into, and out of, a wide deep ditch (dry stream bed). You now continue with the fence on your left for a while, and then aim towards the (**Ulpham**) farm buildings ahead on the right, between some trees. Go through a metal gate in the wall and follow the markings around to the left, through two more gates (one wooden and one metal) to reach a track. Cross this and go through another metal gate, past **Batey Shield Farm** on the left and into a field (stunted trees and a fence on your left), which may have practice jumps for horses in it. Keep to the left edge of the field. At the end is a wooden footbridge over the **Kellah Burn** with a wooden step stile at the entrance.

Cross the bridge (there is a PW signpost with yellow chevrons just after the bridge) to reach a tarmac road. Go up the track ahead to **Greenriggs**. Go into the cluttered yard (don't go round it or you will either have to retrace your steps or cross a barbed wire fence to regain the path) and ahead to a ladder stile, in the right corner of the back yard, which you should cross. After heavy rain it can be very waterlogged on the other side of this stile. After the stile, walk NNW uphill through rough pasture to reach a small ladder stile in a wire fence partially hidden in the rushes. There is a slab on either side of the stile and an acorn on one of the uprights.

Ahead of you is Round Hill where it is very easy to get mis-placed, as there are quite a few sheep tracks that resemble paths and there is virtually no signage.

Continue in the same direction for about 150 yards then bear left (W) on a faint path in the grass. After about 400 yards, you should pass an old quarry on your left, and meet a wire fence. If you are at the right spot, you will find a short marker post by the fence with an acorn and a yellow directional arrow directing you to turn right along the fence. If you miss this point and meet the fence at another point, just turn right at the fence and walk with the fence on your left. There should be a faint path alongside the fence.

This part of the Pennine Way along the fence almost always seems to be wet underfoot. You will just have to grin and bear it.

Go down into, and out of a dip, still with the fence on your left. You will soon come to a small wooden bridge with a white acorn on the left side. Cross this and continue ahead to the top of the next slope. You will next meet a ladder stile in a wall ahead, with a boggy area in front of it. There is, however, a short section of duckboards which may help keep your feet dry. Cross the stile and bear left towards the corner of the fence on your left. There is a small indistinct ruin here marked as '**Eadleystone**' on the OS maps. At the fence corner, bear left and head up the slope towards a stone wall. Keep the trig point (S 6267) on **Black Hill**, which is visible over the wall, to your left as you approach the wall and cross the ladder stile over it, (with care as it can be very slippery in wet weather!). Continue slightly right ahead and descend to a wooden step stile with a grab post in the wire fence ahead. In the distance, down the slope are two slightly ruined quarry buildings (**Gap Shields Fan**). The taller building on the left has a red rusty roof. You need to walk down the slope, to the right of these buildings. You may be able to see a light green grassy path through the rough pasture after the buildings. This is what you are aiming for. After you pass them, a few slabs underfoot guide you. Continue in the same direction to meet a track with a metal gate in the fence on your right. There is a PW signpost here.

Section 14.5

Turn right (E) to go through the metal gate and follow the green track, passing under some power lines and later a small derelict shed (it used to have half a red roof in 2011 but alas this has now gone) on your right after several hundred yards. A few yards after this, go through the wooden gate across the track (or use the ladder stile). Shortly after, you pass some old grass covered mine workings (tips) on the right. Very soon after this, you come to a PW signpost, where you cross a wooden step stile on the left and go along another wide track which curves to the left, under power lines, and through a wooden gate or the wooden step stile next to it. You next meet some trees on the right, go through a metal gate and then descend down to a set of double metal gates and the very busy **A69** road. A wooden side gate gives walkers access to the road. There is a stone PW marker pointing back (for the benefit of north to south walkers) as well as a PW signpost with the finger post pointing back the way you have just come. This road always has a stream of cars and lorries speeding past so you will need to take great care when you cross it. It is strange to see such a sight after the quiet of the moors. On the other side is another PW signpost and wooden steps up the embankment on the other side. At the top you cross the old (abandoned) road into **Greenhead** (the **A69** now bypasses **Greenhead**) to a stile with a PW map board to the left of it.

If time is short take this road into **Greenhead**, and retrace your steps back the following morning, otherwise follow the directions below.

Cross the wooden stile and the metal gate immediately in front of it. Now go diagonally right across the field to a stile in the wall. Cross and continue ahead to a second stile in a second wall.

On your right is the local Haltwhistle golf course so keep an eye open for stray golf balls (on the PW not on the golf course!). These can be handed in at the hotel as you don't want to carry them back home with you, do you?

Now, with a fence and a wall on your right, continue ahead until you come to a PW signpost next to a ladder stile. Cross over the stile. The 3rd green is on the right. Go straight ahead and later cross a two plank wooden footbridge with a guide rail on the left, and a white acorn and yellow directional arrow on the upright.

As you walk across the golf course, on your left, is a ditch, which is actually Roman in origin. It is the **Vallum**, a defensive ditch dug to protect the Wall (this merits a capital letter because it is **Hadrian's Wall**). Away to your right on the golf course, according to the OS map, is the site of a Roman Camp.

Continue ahead. On your left, **Thirlwall Castle** comes into view. At a PW signpost, go left, down quite a steep bank to a small wooden gate and PW signpost to the road (**B6318**). Cross the road to a metal gate on the other side. There is a PW signpost here (National Trails. **Thirlwall Castle** ¼; **Walltown Quarry** 1). Go through this to a fenced grass path in front of a row of cottages (built in 1907 for colliery workers). At the end of the path and the cottages is a wooden kissing gate. There is a white acorn on the gate post. More importantly is a sign which says 'Stop, Look, Listen. Beware of trains'. On the other side of the kissing gate is the railway line between Carlisle and Newcastle. Cross this with care! On the other side is another kissing gate with a white acorn, and visible ahead is a wooden footbridge (white acorn on one of the uprights) over the **Pow Charney Burn**.

Here you have a choice of two routes into **Greenhead**. Just before you reach the burn is a finger post on the right, which says 'Public Footpath **Greenhead** ½'. Immediately below it is another sign for the youth hostel in **Greenhead**. This takes you down a narrow path with the **Tipalt Burn** and 2-bar wooden fence on the side next to the burn and a tall wooden fence on the other side. This path brings you into **Greenhead** by the hostel. On the other side of the burn is a tarmac access road reached via a wooden kissing gate on the right and a narrow wooden bridge with wooden railings on both sides. This is Cycle Route 68 which you can follow into **Greenhead** too and it too comes out by the hostel.

These are your exit points for the PW into **Greenhead**. You will need to retrace your steps tomorrow to continue your walk northwards. In **Greenhead** there is the Greenhead Hotel, the Old Forge Tearooms, the Greenhead Hostel plus a phone box. The same people own both the hotel and the hostel so you will need to go into the hotel to book in. There is a B&B and camping barn by **Thirlwall Castle** and a B&B on the **B6318** outside **Greenhead** (when you descended to the **B6318** from the golf course, turn left up the road and it is on the right).

Opposite the church, over the road facing the burn is the (small) Millennium Green, where a (now rather faded) millennium plaque set into the green as part of the 2000 AD celebrations has an image of a PW signpost, a bobble hat and a boot.

Section 15 – Greenhead to Once Brewed

Distance – 6.7 miles / 10.7 km (PW route only)
Height gained on PW route – 400 m (1,312 ft)
Height lost on PW route – 275 m (902 ft)

Route outline: Greenhead to Thirlwall Castle; Walltown Quarry; Walltown Crags; Turret 44B; Cockmount Hill Farm; Great Chesters Fort and Farm; Cawfields Quarry; Milecastle 42; Caw Gap; Milecastle 41; Winshield Crags; Steel Rigg; Once Brewed.

Hadrian's Wall near Walltown Quarry
(the Wall negates the need for signage here!)

Section 15.1

If you stayed overnight at **Greenhead**, return to the PW where it crosses the **Pow Charney Burn**. After crossing the wooden footbridge over the **Pow Charney Burn**, bear left to a gate with the **Tipalt Burn** on your right. Continue on a grassy path with a fence on the left and trees on the right.

> Ahead appears the substantial ruined remains of **Thirlwall Castle**. Thirlwall means 'gap in the wall'. This 14th Century Pele Tower was constructed about 1346 from stones taken from the Wall. It is open, with no entrance fee and well worth a stop to explore it.

The path ends at a small new wooden gate in front of a track. Immediately ahead is **Thirlwall Castle**. Turn right on the track and cross the **Tipalt Burn** once again via a stone footbridge, passing **Holmhead** B&B on your right. Go up a walled lane, which climbs and bends to the left to reach a wooden gate in a stone wall. Go through the gate and walk up the slope, with a ditch and stone wall on your right.

> The ditch is the **Vallum**, which you last saw on the golf course yesterday. If you look back, you can see the castle though the trees, as well as the row of cottages and the golf course.

At the top of the slope is a wall with a short 3-step ladder stile, which you cross.

> On the right (S) is the site of Milecastle 46. A little further south is the site of Magnis Roman Fort (Carvoran).

Continue ahead in the same direction, to a wooden kissing gate, which has slabs leading up to it and beyond. Ahead is a tarmac road. There is a PW signpost here (**Thirlwall** ¾; **Cawfields Quarry** 3¼).

Section 15.2

Go through the kissing gate and turn right on the road for a short distance, before turning left into the car park of the old **Walltown Quarry**.

> The extraction of whinstone from the quarry ceased in 1978 and it is now disused and landscaped. There is a café here, toilets, and visitors' centre.

Whinstone chip paths abound here but the PW one has stubby guide-posts with white acorns and yellow directional arrows to guide you on your way. The path initially has a wall on the right and an escarpment (**Rabbit Heugh**) on the left, then later has fences on both sides, and then becomes open as it crosses the centre of the old quarry.

> When I first walked the PW in the mid 1970s, this was a working quarry, with all the dust and noise associated with it and it was quarrying stone including the Wall itself. It even removed Roman Wall Turret (45B)! The Roman Wall was designated a UNESCO World Heritage Site in 1987, and is thus heavily protected. Where you could once walk along the top of parts of the Wall, this is no longer allowed, apart from a small section near Housesteads, which isn't on the Pennine Way anyway, but well worth a visit if you have the time. The AD122 bus will take you there and back (entrance fee). As this is a short day, why not take advantage of seeing as much of the Roman artefacts concentrated within this area, such as Housesteads or Vindolanda.

Head up towards the cliff at the end of the quarry, ignoring another path, which joins it from the right. Just before the cliff the path is fenced on both sides and swings right and ascends in an arc to a kissing gate, with a wooden bench next to it, if you need a rest. Here you turn left to make the final ascent to the top of the quarry and **Hadrian's Wall**, named after Emperor Hadrian Aelius (AD 97 to 117), is reached at last!

You are now on **Walltown Crags** and the next section of the Wall is arguably one of the best sections of it that you will see (demonstrated in the photograph at the start of this section). Don't expect to see the Wall as the Romans left it. Most of it was grubbed down to ground level over the centuries as the locals used the conveniently pre-cut Roman stones for house building etc. What you see now is a reconstruction, but it is impressive nevertheless. Some guide books refer to the 'Clayton Wall' on this section and what you see on today's walk, is largely due to one man, John Clayton, who realised the importance of the Wall and, when he inherited his father's estate in the 19th Century, he bought up most of the farms along the line of the Wall between his estate near Chollerford and Cumbria, which stopped the Wall being dismantled for its stone. If you walk the Wall in its entirety, you will realise that there is far less of the Wall visible on the ground than you would expect. It has been build over, it forms part of our road system, and in places it has been grubbed out so that only the grassed over foundations remain, sometimes invisible on the ground.

The Wall is 73 miles long, or 80 Roman miles, as a Roman mile has 1,620 yards. The word 'mile' comes from the Latin word 'mille', meaning 1,000, as 1,620 yards is the equivalent of a 1,000 double-step marching paces by Roman soldiers. Most of the Wall was completed in six years. The work was carried out by three Roman legions, of 5,000 men each – the XX Valeria, VI Victrix and II Augusta. They built the Wall to a height of 20 feet and made it 10 feet thick in places (the Broad Wall). Each of the 25 million (or so) facing stones were 10 inches long, 6 inches high, and 20 inches deep and quarried locally. Milecastles, housing 32 men, were built into the wall (80 in all) and between each milecastle were two turrets, or observation towers (shown as A and B on OS maps), with 10 men. There were also 16 forts along the wall, (normally 7 miles apart) housing between 500 and 1,000 men. A very impressive undertaking indeed! Roman legions built the Wall but it was manned by auxiliary legions from Europe who came from places as far apart as Belgium and Iraq. They had to earn their Roman citizenship through their military service. The numbering system of the Wall was the work of Professor R. G. Collingwood. Milecastles and turrets are numbered from east to west so milecastle 45 is 45 Roman miles (41 miles / 66 km) from the eastern end of the Wall at Wallsend. Roman soldiers finally left Britain in AD 409.

The section of the PW between **Walltown Crags** and **Steel Rigg**, where you leave the Wall for the night at Once Brewed (your overnight stop), is fairly straightforward because you walk with the Wall on your left. The section before **Walltown Crags**, just after the quarry, is very impressive. The Wall is built on an escarpment of Whin Sill (last seen on the River Tees) and there are steep drops on the northern side of the Wall in places. There are also a lot of ups and downs, which is why it is better to spend a separate day walking along the Wall rather than add it onto an already long day from **Alston**, or extend the day to **Bellingham**. You may not come this way again so it would be a pity to rush it. On some of the crags, you can look down onto the Wall and milecastles, which are very photogenic.

After the first 'dip' in the Wall, you come to the ruins of **Turret 45A**, which has a little map board beside it giving you some of the history of it.

It is interesting to note that this turret was here before the Wall was built as you can clearly see that the Wall was built up to the turret, then continued on the other side rather than the turret being built into the Wall as many others are. It would have originally been a watchtower, or signal station, and as it was pre-Wall, it is also less than the standard ⅓ mile from Milecastle 45.

After this section of Wall, the Wall surprisingly disappears and all that is left is a low grassy bank with stones on it and a wire fence to keep you (and any animals) from straying over the edge. If you look (carefully) over the wire fence you can see an old flooded Roman quarry.

At the end of **Walltown Crags** is a dip, with a rough track in it. Ahead you can see the foundations of the Wall, and to the right, flag stones appear once again. Descend into the dip, crossing a track, where flagstones appear underfoot, to reach and cross a ladder stile in the wall ahead. Ascend up the other side to the top of the crag on more flagstones. As you climb the slope, you come to **Turret 44B (King Arthur's Turret)**. From here there is a great view back along the section you have just walked. The farm that you can see (looking back) on the left is Walltown Farm. Continue up the slope. There is another dip, before you climb another crag, and descend to a ladder stile in a wall. On a grassy path you continue to a stone step stile in a wall, with a carved acorn on one of the wall stones. Soon an ordinary farm wall replaces the Wall foundations on your left. Oh what a disappointment when you have experienced the real thing! You continue on gently sloping ground with two plantations visible ahead. Just before the plantation, look carefully at the wooden gate in the wall on your left. The rounded stone gatepost on the left side is in fact a Roman Milestone!

Section 15.3

Cross the ladder stile ahead and walk through the narrow plantation, crossing a second ladder stile to exit it. You next pass **Cockmount Hill Farm** with its small walled garden on the left. Ahead in the distance you can see another, more substantial farm. To the right of that farm is **Aesica Roman Fort (Great Chesters)**. Continue ahead to a ladder stile in a wall and cross this. Head for the gap in the bank ahead which crosses your path. Once through it, you are in **Great Chesters**.

Aesica was a small infantry fort, and was probably an after-thought (demonstrated by the fact that the remains of Milecastle 43 lie beneath the NW corner of the fort).

The most interesting thing to see here now, is in the corner diagonally right (SE). It is a Roman Altar (or a copy – you can never be sure!) and it usually has a good supply of small coins on it – presumably visitors' offerings to the Roman gods! The altar has a wine flagon carved on it. To the right of the altar are 3 stones, two on the base and one on top. If you look very carefully at the topmost stone, you can see that it has a carving of a Roman soldier holding a shield at arms length. It is difficult to make out because of all the lichen and discolouration to the stone. You will also see the ruins of barrack blocks and there is a vaulted arch in the fenced in section near the path.

You leave the fort by crossing a second ladder stile in the wall by the farmhouse. A hundred yards or so along the outside of this wall is a very faded rectangular (white coloured) Roman dedication stone. Not much to look at, but Roman remains nevertheless. Continue with the farm wall on your left to a short ladder stile in a wall ahead. Cross a second ladder stile in a second wall (ahead you can see **Cawfields Quarry** and a road going off to the right, which goes to the Milecastle Inn, which is on the AD122 bus route). Walk down the slope and pass **Burnhead** B&B on your left.

The grass along the path here is usually kept quite short by constant mowing. A reminder that about a third of the National Trail's budget for Hadrian's Wall is spent on keeping vegetation down. Another interesting fact is that the section of Hadrian's Wall which runs parallel with the Pennine Way is managed by the Hadrian's Wall National Trail Officer because of the special historical nature of the route.

Continue down the slope and over a stone step stile to the road (in the summer, the bank ahead on the right is usually a mass of purple plants called Rosebay Willowherb). There is a National Trails signpost by the stile (**Walltown Quarry** 3¾). Turn right on the tarmac road, over the bridge crossing **Caw Burn,** then turn left at the fork in the road to reach a car park on the right and public toilets. The PW signpost here says **Steel Rigg** 2¾.

Next to the car park is an old quarry, which, when it was in use, up until 1944, cut through a section of the Wall and part of the Whin Sill escarpment. The old quarry site is now flooded and forms a lake, and behind it is the inverted 'V' of Whin Sill left behind. The dolerite extracted from the quarry was used in road building. This is a good place for a break, particularly in view of the fact that public toilets are rare on the PW.

Section 15.4

You leave the car park via a cinder path on the left side of the lake. There is a stone wall on the right of the path initially which takes you to a wooden kissing gate. Go through it and follow the path up the hill to a second kissing gate built into the Wall (here the PW goes left but it is worth following the slope, and the Wall up to your right as it gives a good aerial photograph of the Milecastle). Turn left, with the Wall on your left and walk up to the remains of **Milecastle 42**.

Milecastle 42 was built on a slope, which must have been very uncomfortable for the Roman auxiliaries who would have manned it. There is a really good section of Wall between here and **Caw Gap** so have your cameras ready. Somewhere between these two points is supposedly a swastika (a Roman symbol of prosperity) on one of the Wall stones but I have never found it. That doesn't stop me looking each time I pass this way though.

After the Milecastle there is a short section next to the Wall that is fenced off. You can enter it via gates at both ends if you wish. Further along the Wall, just after **Thorny Doors**, where there is a small wooden gate in the Wall, the path goes up a slope using stone steps in the turf with a gate at the end. At the top is a tall marker post, and several small ones further on. The Wall is low enough to sit on here (if this is allowed on a World Heritage Site!). Soon after there is a dip in the Wall called **Bloody Gap**. You cross a stile in a wooden fence that crosses the path and then descend towards **Turret 41A**. Somewhere behind you is **Turret 41B** but it is not visible on the ground. You now descend to a gate (with a National Trails signpost – **Cawfields Quarry** 1) where you cross a tarmac road at **Caw Gap** (there is a good aerial view looking back along the Wall from the crag on the other side the road).

Section 15.5

Go through the gate (another National Trails signpost – **Steel Rigg** 1¾; Housesteads 4¾) on the other side of the road and up some steps. The Wall disappears here. On your left is now a stone wall with some Roman stones used in its construction in some sections, making it look like a slimmed down Roman Wall. You unknowingly pass the site of **Milecastle 41** on the way up the slope to a wooden gate in a wall ahead. The path undulates with the terrain. You later pass a rather windswept tree on the left, and continue up the slope to go through a second gate. Soon after you come to a signpost for Winshields Campsite (and bunkhouse) and Tea Room. Ignore this (unless you are staying there) and continue up the slope to the trig point (S 6489), on **Winshield Crags**, which becomes visible ahead. This is the highest point on the Wall at 345 metres (1,230 feet).

> There used to be a pay to use (20p) telescope here many years ago (like the ones you still get at the seaside) but it has since been removed. It is, however, a reminder that this is another of those times when you should have your camera ready. On a clear sunny day, the view ahead towards **Peel Crags** and **Highshield Crags**, with **Crag Lough** next to it, is probably the best long distance view you will ever get on the PW section of the Wall.

The Wall reappears for a short section before being replaced by a stone wall, built on the foundations of the Roman Wall. Go through a gate in a wall, which crosses the path. Here, stop and have a look over the wall and along it. You should be able to see a Roman ditch on the other side of the wall heading into some trees. Go down the slope to a second gate in a wall ahead. Just before are the non-visible remains of **Milecastle 40**. Continue down the slope to a third gate and a tarmac road. The National Trails signpost here says **Caw Gap** 1¾. You are now at **Steel Rigg** and should turn right down the road to the Once Brewed youth hostel or the Twice Brewed Inn for the night.

You will need to return to this spot tomorrow to continue your walk. There is a bus stop by the hostel where you can get the AD122 bus (named after the year the Wall was commissioned) to Vindolanda if you have time, or you could walk the 1¼ miles each way if you feel fit. It is mooted to be the most important Roman site in Britain because of the discovery by Robin Birley in 1973 of the Vindolanda postcards (wooden writing tablets used by the Romans), leather sandals and various other Roman arte-facts beautifully preserved in the peat. The museum there has many fascinating pieces and although the actual postcards are in the British Museum in London, photographs of the original are at Vindolanda. There are also substantial Roman remains at Vindolanda and a full size model of part of the Wall, in addition to the museum. There is a charge to enter the site.

Section 16 - Once Brewed to Bellingham

Distance – 14.6 miles / 23.6 km (PW route only)
Height gained on PW route – 520 m (1,708 ft)
Height lost on PW route – 655 m (2,150 ft)

Route outline: Once Brewed to Steel Rigg; Sycamore Gap; Crag Lough; Hotbank Crags; Rapishaw Gap; Wark Forest; Sell Burn; Ladyhill; Warks Burn; Horneystead Farm; The Ash; Leadgate Cottage; Lowstead; Houxty Burn; Shitlington Crags; B6320; River North Tyne; Bellingham.

Wark Forest South

Section 16.1

Walk back up the tarmac road to **Steel Rigg**. At the National Trail signpost on the right, (opposite the exit point from the path yesterday), cross the low wall on the right using the stone step stile in the wall. Walk to the wooden gate in the stone wall ahead and go through.

Note that the Wall here (which is on your right as, unusually, you are on the north side of the Wall at this point) has a grassy top. Walkers used to be able to walk on some sections of the Wall (this being one of them) and there used to be wooden steps up to the Wall and off it again, to allow you access to the Wall. This privilege has since been withdrawn, but the grassy tops remain. There is a good view of **Crag Lough** and **Hotbank Farm** ahead.

Turn right after the gate and go downhill (Wall on your right) on a grassy path, that joins a flagged path (from a gate in the Wall above), which leads to a relatively recent renovated section of the Roman Wall. Note there is a gap in the Wall where it bends left towards the short renovated section.

There is a turret on the other side of the renovated Wall, which is strange as the site of **Turret 39B** is just before the **Peel** road and the site of **Turret 39A** is on **Peel Crags** which is ahead of you. The OS map is as confused about this as I am and simply says 'Turret' or 'Tower', rather than giving it a number and letter. There are therefore three turrets on this section of the Wall, which is unique. It has been suggested that for strategic reasons, the Romans required a third turret here, but why only here and not anywhere else on the Wall? I am sure that the archaeologists will say it is Roman in origin but if you are using Roman materials and methods who is to say?

Ascend up the other side of the dip, which is quite steep, on a stepped flagged path to a ladder stile in a wall crossing your path. From the top of the crag (**Peel Crags**) there is a good view back to the turret, Peel Farmhouse, and the Twice Brewed Inn. On the level ground on top of the crag the Wall reappears on your left. The path beside it initially is gravelled. The Wall contains Roman stone but doesn't look quite Roman. You cross another stile in a crossing wall before descending into a dip to reach the very impressive looking **Milecastle 39**, often seen on postcards of the Wall.

Milecastle 39 is impressive because there is a good view of it from above before you actually reach it. You can clearly see the gate in the Wall on the north side of it, with an entrance to the south, which is typical of a Roman milecastle. The corners of milecastles are rounded, which look strange as almost everything else that is Roman on the Wall has sharp corners. There is a flagged path down to the milecastle and it is flagged up the other side of the dip. Up on the top is another set of Roman foundations, not of a turret, which are usually ⅓ of a Roman mile apart, but possibly of officers' quarters (according to Henry Stedman in the Trailblazer guide for *Hadrian's Wall* 2008, p148); another unique feature on this section of the Wall.

Ascend up the slope on a slabbed path, passing the set of Roman foundations. The next descent, which is quite steep, is a bit of a surprise because there is a solitary sycamore tree in the dip, giving it its modern name of **Sycamore Gap**.

The tree was in a walled enclosure in Wainwright's day (1967 p37) but has since outgrown it. It is quite close to the Wall, and its roots must be under the foundations. There is a circular walled enclosure to the right of the tree. The tree was made famous in the film 'Robin Hood Prince of Thieves' with Kevin Cosner and Morgan Freeman. If you want to make a circular walk of this section to Once Brewed, you should walk several yards south from the tree to pick up a nice reasonably level grassy track, (the Roman Military Way), which will take you all the way back to **Steel Rigg**. Turn right on the track and you will come out at Peel Farm. Even if you don't want to do a circular walk, you can get a great photograph of **Sycamore Gap** from just below the circular walled enclosure.

There is supposed to be a swastika stone in the north facing part of the Wall here but, again, despite searching for it every time I go by, I have yet to find it.

Section 16.2

The path crosses a man-made gap in the wall just past the sycamore tree, taking you once again onto the northern side of the Wall, and it then climbs in an arc (with the Wall now on your right) on a stoned path, before returning to the Wall further up the slope. Here it immediately veers left away from the Wall again (to protect this section of the Wall from erosion). At the top of the rise is **Highshield Crags** where you cross a stile in a wall and continue ahead on a flat dirt path with **Crag Lough** far below on your left. There is no fence or wall on your left here so don't stray from the path.

You soon enter some trees, with a wall on your right and descend through the copse, on a stone path, crossing two short ladder stiles to meet a track. There is a signpost here pointing back to **Steel Rigg**, 1½ mile distant. Cross the track to a wooden gate in the wall ahead. There is another signpost here with one finger post pointing right (**Steel Rigg** 1½ via Roman Military Way) and one ahead (National Trails Housesteads 1½). This is **Milking Gap** and the track connects **Hotbank Farm** with the B6318. Go through the small wooden gate ahead (white acorn on the left side of the gate) and uphill on a stony path to a wide grassy track with a stone wall and the farm track on your left. Go past **Hotbank Farm** on this grassy track with a wall on your left and a wire fence on the right. Go through a new kissing gate.

On the northern side of the gate is a wooden plaque with **Milecastle 38** on it. If you look back, you can make out the grassed over foundations of this milecastle to the right of the flagged path you have just walked.

Continue in the same direction, up the slope with the Wall soon joining you on your left. Follow this nice grassy path as it undulates over **Hotbank Crags** beside the Wall. Just before a dip in the path, the Roman Wall, becomes an ordinary wall again, although it looks like

Roman stones have been used in it too. Ahead over the dip, the Wall (grass-topped) continues.

> On your left, over the wall, you should have a good view of the forest that you are heading for next. The building you can see on the forest edge is East Stonefolds. The small white building with no roof, on the edge of a huge field is an old kiln.

Descend on a stone path into the dip, (**Rapishaw Gap**), with **Hotbank Crags** behind and Cuddy's Crags directly in front. This is where we leave the Roman Wall.

Section 16.3

Do not take the short ladder stile, with a wooden platform on top, in the stone wall a few feet in front of you. Instead, cross the ladder stile, next to a wooden gate and PW signpost (**Leadgate** 7¼) in the wall on your left. The lough (lake), visible ahead on the right is **Broomlee Lough**. In front of you is a huge field with (ordinary) stone walls on both sides. Do not take the obvious path along the left wall as this will take you to the old kiln, which is off route (although in Wainwright's day this was actually the line of the PW). Instead, you need to cross the field diagonally (left to right) to a gate and ladder stile in the wall in the far right corner of the field. You should be able to see the faint line of the path and the gate from the Wall. There is a short section of slabs over the boggiest part of the field, with a wooden rail to the left in the middle. The trees ahead are the **Wark Forest**, the largest man-made forest in Europe.

Go through the gate (or cross the ladder stile) and continue in the same direction to a second gate and ladder stile in a wall ahead. Walk to a short guidepost with white acorns and directional arrows on it. This directs you down a track which zigzags down a grassy slope, crossing **Jenkins Burn**. Go ahead (N) on a faint grassy path, veering slightly right, to a wooden kissing gate next to a wooden gate and PW signpost (Pennine Way Public Footpath and yellow chevron). Cross the grassy track here and cross the wooden step stile in the fence on the other side (or walk around it as the fence has gone here), which has a broken people counter on it. The PW signpost directs you half right to a short guidepost, where you turn left and go down a bank, to a slabbed marshy area (the result of a small sike feeding into **Greenlee Lough** on your left).

Go up the slope, past another short guidepost. Keep a sharp eye out for other short guideposts, which will keep you to the correct line (the path is quite faint on this section) across an area of scrubland. Don't cross the wide wooden footbridge over the **Haughtongreen Burn** that you pass on the left (with East Stonefolds Farm in line with it). Instead continue with the burn on your left towards a wall ahead. Before you reach the wall, you pass through a gap in a wall (passing a now surplus wooden ladder stile with a yellow directional arrow on it) and a few yards ahead you cross a second footbridge, which has a grab rail on the left of it. Turn half left up the slope towards a guidepost, which you should be able to see on the horizon ahead, cutting off a kink in the wall. Then, with the wall on your right, continue to a short ladder stile by a gap in a wall ahead, (with a PW signpost), and walk down the slope to a small wooden bridge with a handrail on the right, to a forestry track. There is a two-finger PW signpost here. Both finger posts have a yellow chevron and say 'Pennine Way Public Footpath'.

Turn right on the gravel track and go through a wooden gate (old ladder stile to the right) and follow the track into the forest (**Wark Forest South**). At a fork, go left, still on the main track. Ignore a track on the left further up. You next come to a cross track (Robinrock 3¾ miles left; Haughton Green ½ mile right) where you continue ahead, down a dip and up again. Ignore a second track on the left.

Soon after, at a PW signpost (see photograph at the beginning of this section), turn half right on a muddy path, which will take you into the forest. The path is relatively easy to follow with short guideposts with white acorns and yellow directional arrows here and there, but it can be quite boggy because of the trees. To the left of one of the short guideposts (which has D 73162 stencilled on it) over some ferns, is a guidepost with a finger post pointing back to Bellcrag Flow. Eventually a large clearing opens up on the right of the path (**Haughton Common**).

You can see more trees at the far end of the clearing. This is **Wark Forest Central**. Just before the forest, a small walled plantation with a few trees should also be visible. You will pass to the left of this soon.

Section 16.4

You leave the trees at a wooden gate with a wooden step stile on the left. It is very boggy on the approach to the gate. Cross the stile and head across the clearing (in a north easterly direction) on a green path. There are few features here. One is a wooden step stile to the left of a gate in a fence, which crosses the path. A few yards later you cross **Sell Burn** in the dip ahead, and head towards the walled plantation, which is directly ahead. When you get there, if the weather is favourable, this is a good place for a break as it is drier here than the surrounding area. Ahead are lots of gloomy conifers with wet paths underfoot. You continue on the boggy path towards the forest to a wooden gate in a wire fence, with a wooden stile on the right and a very moss covered PW signpost between the two.

Here time has come full circle as the section of forest in front of the fence was felled in 2012. In earlier editions of Wainwright's excellent *Pennine Way Companion*, he mentioned that this section was felled in 1967 (p33).

Go over the stile and descend on a green track, with felled areas on both sides, to cross a well-maintained forest track in front of **Wark Forest Central**. A short guidepost with a yellow directional arrow encourages you to continue ahead down the slope, on an obvious path, with trees on your right and a cleared triangle of tree stumps on your left. You soon come out onto another track where a PW signpost directs you to turn right along the track for a short distance. Leave the track, turning half left at another PW signpost, descending on a very grassy path, crossing **Gofton Burn** on a wooden footbridge with a guide rail on the left. There is a white acorn on the upright to reassure you that you are still on the PW. Still heading approximately NNE through the forest you cross another forest track (short guidepost) and continue down the slope through the forest to another track, again with a short guidepost with a white acorn and yellow directional arrow as a guide.

Cross the track and continue ahead in the same direction. Soon a low, sometimes crumbly wall appears on the right of the path, and it becomes much drier underfoot. Ahead half right, a farmstead can be seen. Follow the wall down, trees on the left and open grassland on the right, passing through a wooden kissing gate in a four-bar wooden fence. Here the trees end but the wall continues on your right. You descend down a grassy slope towards a tarmac road.

Section 16.5

In the wall corner you cross a wooden fence via a wooden step stile with a grab post and white acorn on it. A PW signpost, on the other side of the fence, between a wooden gate and the stile, directs you right along the tarmac road, passing the entrance to **Willowbog Farm** on the left. Opposite the entrance to **Ladyhill** on the right, at a PW signpost, turn left down a wide grassy path with a dry stone wall on the left and trees on the right.

Note that here the finger post is the first one that has a red chevron on it, indicating that this section of the PW is a BOAT (Byway Open to All Traffic). The section of the wall by the road has slabs on it, forming a seat, if you want to take a rest here.

The path takes you to another tarmac road. Here there is a double PW finger post with red chevrons on both. Cross the road and continue ahead in the same direction, crossing a gravel track, after which the path veers half right and enters a short section of forest. Unfortunately, when I was here in late 2012, the ground underfoot had been churned up into a deep muddy mess by the passage of one or several trail bikes. Hopefully this should have been remedied by the time you walk it, as it has been scheduled for repair. At the end of the short section of enclosed trees is a wooden gate between two stone gateposts. Go over the wooden step stile on the left of the gate.

You now cross open countryside again. Short guideposts with white acorns and yellow directional arrows will guide you here so keep a sharp eye out for them. The path heads roughly NE at first. **Fawlee Sike** appears on the left, and the path goes more NNE, and then descends towards the sike, as the sike curves to the right, and the PW crosses it. The path goes up the slope on the other side towards a wall corner. Keep the wall on your left and continue to a gate where the wall bends right ahead. Go through the gate, or use the ladder stile next to it, and go downhill through tussocks and rushes. Ahead, slightly to the right is a corrugated iron hut in front of a tree. On the hill above, half right of the tin hut, is **Horneystead Farm**. Continue down the grassy slope, (towards **Warks Burn** in the tree-lined dip ahead), with a wire fence a few yards away on your right. The wire fence is replaced by a dry stone wall and after a few yards you reach a ladder stile over the wall on your right. There is a blue metal gate here and an old moss covered PW signpost with a modification order dating back to 2007 nailed to the upright post.

Go over the stile, or through the gate, and pass the corrugated iron hut on your left. Go past it for about 100 yards and then go down a slope to a gap in the bank on the left. There is a short guidepost here. Go through the gap, down the bank and bear left, through the ferns, to reach a concrete and metal footbridge, with a wooden gate with a white acorn on it at the front. Cross the footbridge over **Warks Burn**. Someone with a sense of humour has nailed a yellow diamond shaped warning sign to a tree on the other side of the burn which says 'Danger Crocodiles. No Swimming'.

Section 16.6

Climb up the slope on the path to a small rock outcrop where you turn right, with the path, and cross a field on a faint path over rough pasture to reach a wooden step stile in a wire fence (acorn and yellow arrow on the right support below the grab post) on the skyline. The farm half left across the field in front is **Horneystead**. Continue ahead, to the farm track, passing the farm on your left in the process. There is a metal gate across the track (wooden step stile on the left) in front of a couple of wooden pylons. At the PW signpost, leave the track before it bends sharp left, and continue ahead towards a wall in the distance. Cross a wooden step stile, in a short section of wooden fencing next to a wire fence, before you reach the wall. Cross the wall using the stone steps. Go diagonally right and through another gate in the wall. The building away on the left is **The Ash**. Turn left and walk with the wall on your left for several yards to a wooden kissing gate. Go through this and cross the meadow with **The Ash** still on your left, to cross a ladder stile (or go through the wooden gate) near the wall corner. Walk ahead around the farmstead, through a metal gate next to the boundary wall, then with a wall and tarmac road on your left, walk to the stile in the wire fence ahead (next to a metal gate) in front of the road. **Leadgate Cottage** is the building on the left of the stile. There is a PW sign here with mileage again. **Rapishaw Gap** is 7¼ miles behind and **Bellingham** (pronounced 'Belling jam') is 5¼ miles ahead. Cross the stile, the road, and another stile on the other side.

The path bends left after the stile, along rough pasture with a wire fence on your left, almost hidden in the rushes. Head towards a short ladder stile in the dry stone wall ahead. You now head half right up the slope towards the edge of the line of trees ahead. When you reach the trees there is a short finger post with an acorn and directional arrow. The stone building ahead is **Lowstead**. Follow a broad green path in a slight left curve towards **Lowstead**.

Once upon a time the PW went into the garden of **Lowstead** via a wooden step stile in the fence and exited at a gate by the side of the house.

In recent years (probably caused by a change in owners who wanted more privacy!) the PW now follows a path anticlockwise around the building and exits down some steps onto the driveway in front of the house.

Section 16.7

From here, the navigation is much easier. After reaching the driveway, turn right and walk on the tarmac road away from the house, over a cattle grid. The road bends to the right, through the gate, past a turning on the left, over a second cattle grid, to an angled T-junction. There is a PW signpost with red chevrons (Pennine Way Public Byway) here, which also has a Cycle Route 68 sign attached (last seen at **Greenhead**).

Turn left, still on the road, uphill initially, over a third cattle grid, and down the slope to a second T-junction. Here you leave the tarmac and continue ahead, over the wooden step stile (white acorn) in a wooden four-bar fence between the wooden gate on its left and the

PW signpost with a red chevron, and cycle route 68 signpost on its right. Continue ahead, along the side of a field, with a wire fence and some stunted hawthorn trees on your right.

> The farm ahead on the left has the delightful name of **Shitlington Hall**, and you will pass by it on your way to the equally delightfully named **Shitlington Crags**. The ridge ahead with a relay station (mast) on the top is **Ealingham Rigg.**

Towards the end of the field a short guidepost directs you left, (you head towards the right edge of the farm buildings ahead in the distance, towards a PW signpost in front of the line of trees along the burn) down the bank to a narrow stone footbridge with metal railings, over **Houxty Burn**. Cross the bridge and turn right, with the burn on your right. Go over a second, smaller footbridge, where the path bends round to the left through a gate and up a track passing **Shitlington Hall Farm** on your left. At the PW signpost (Stone House ¾), go through a second gate, and go along a muddy track, to another gate in the wire fence on the right.

Go through the metal gate and up the slope, with a fence on your right. Cross a small stream (**Slade Sike**), go through another metal gate ahead, and continue up the slope. The fence on your right becomes a wall. At the top, where you reach a wall, it is enclosed on three sides (wooden fence on the right and dry stone walls to your left and ahead). Cattle have churned up the ground here. Go through a metal gate in the wall (or use the wooden ladder stile to the right), cross a track (Shitlington Crag bunkhouse on the left), and go up a grassy track towards the crags ahead. The track bends left and goes through a nick in the crags. There is a short guidepost at the top. You now follow the grassy path through the rough pasture with the metal WT relay mast (it looks like a pylon with a large cigarette sticking out of the top) half right on top of the ridge. Continue on the grassy path to the top of the ridge and cross the dry stone wall ahead using the wooden ladder stile. The PW signpost here (**Shitlington Hall** ¾) directs you to turn right along the top of the ridge (**Ealingham Rigg**), past the mast.

Continue on the track, through a gate and at a PW signpost, you should head north east on a faint narrow path across the moor. However you need to pause here to ensure that you have found your first short guidepost before you head off, as the reeds are as tall as the guideposts, initially making them difficult to spot. Once on the path, head over the moor and cross two sections of duckboards before you reach a tall guidepost with an acorn and yellow directional arrow. The path before you reach the tall guidepost is on fairly flat featureless terrain. Here you get your first glimpse of **Bellingham**. Just keep going in the same direction down the slope, and you will eventually come to the corner of a road, where there is a ladder stile and a PW guidepost.

In poor weather, remember that the road will be on your right and about 300 yards to your left (out of sight) is a wall. If you drift too far to the right, follow the road down to the corner. If you drift too far to the left, follow the wall, and where it bends right, continue with it until you find the short ladder stile in the wall with a PW signpost next to it. Alternatively, you could continue on the track along **Ealingham Rigg** to the road, turn left along it and reach the wall corner that way. At the stile is an advertisement for the bunkhouse in **Bellingham**. From the stile **Bellingham** is clearly visible ahead of you.

Cross the stile and turn left down the minor road, round the bend and several yards later, at a PW signpost, cross the ladder stile in the wall on your left to go diagonally (half right) across rough pasture, over a wooden step stile in a wooden fence which crosses your path (grab post and PW signpost on the left of the stile), and down to a wooden stile and PW signpost in the corner of a fence on the **B6320** road.

Turn left on the road, past Bellingham Camping and Caravan Club (on the left), and the church (on the right) to cross the road bridge over the **River North Tyne**. Note the old tollbooth on the left as you cross the bridge. Just after you cross the narrow road bridge, cross the road, with care, and follow a riverside path which brings you into the village. At the minor road, turn left, past **Lyndale Guesthouse** (on the left) and the **Rose and Crown** (on the right) to a minor square where there is a bakery and the **Rocky Road Café**. Turn left here to the main road. Turn right on the road (**B6320**) past the **Co-op stores**. (Lynn View B&B is ahead up the main road on the right, just before the road bends left). Turn right by Barclays Bank and **Demesne Bunkhouse** (YHA) and Campsite is 75 yards on the right.

Section 17 – Bellingham to Byrness

Distance – 15.1 miles / 24.4 km
Height gained on PW route – 555 m (1,821 ft)
Height lost on PW route – 445 m (1,460 ft)

Route outline: Bellingham to Blakelaw Farm; Hazel Burn; Hareshaw House; B6320; Lough Shaw; Deer Play; Whitley Pike; Brownrigg Head; Redesdale Forest; Blakehopeburnhaugh; River Rede; Byrness Church; A68; Byrness.

Grouse moors between Lough Shaw and Deer Play

Before you leave **Bellingham**, remember that this is the last shopping opportunity that you will have before the end of the walk. There are no shops or banks in **Byrness** or **Kirk Yetholm** itself (although there is a small shop in Town Yetholm opposite the Plough Hotel) so unless your B&B providers will cater for all your food needs, make use of the chemist, the well-stocked Co-op, Barclays bank etc either the night before or on the morning of your departure from **Bellingham**. If you have a bit of time, have a look at the grassy mound of Bellingham Castle in Russell Terrace, just around the corner from the bunkhouse, or the old railway station in Woodburn Road where there are a couple of restored railway carriages in the old station car park (now a heritage centre). **Bellingham** was on the route between Hexham and Riccarton Junction where you could connect with Carlisle or Edinburgh. It opened in 1861, closed to passenger traffic in October 1956 and was closed to all traffic on 11 November 1963. The station was originally known as Bellingham but LNER added the suffix 'North Tyne' to avoid confusion with Bellingham on the Southern Railway. The old station sign is now in the railway museum in York.

Section 17.1

After passing **Demesne Farm** bunkhouse on the right, the road forks. Take the left fork and go up the hill.

Just before the caravan site on the left is what looks like an old village hall. This is the old youth hostel which has been replaced by the bunkhouse. Another sad reminder that every hostel has to make an individual profit in order to survive these days.

When the road bends right, by a covered reservoir with a weather station on top, turn left, through a metal gate and go up the farm road to **Blakelaw Farm**, which is visible in the distance. There is a PW signpost here (**Byrness** 14¼). When you reach the farmyard, turn left, and go through a gate, passing the farmhouse on the left. At the end of a short walled lane, go through a second gate where there is a PW signpost directing you half right up the hill through a pasture towards a prominent PW signpost on the skyline ahead. Once you reach this, head for a shorter guidepost in the same direction. It has a white acorn and a blue directional arrow within a yellow circle. Go past a wall corner on your right to a third guidepost. You now continue up the slope to a wooden gate in the wall ahead. There is a PW signpost here. Continue ahead on a faint path.

The white building in the far distance, surrounded by trees is **Hareshaw House**, our next objective. The route between the gate and the house can be awkward to follow in places so you will need to pay attention to the ground ahead.

After a short while the next landmark appears. This is a very mossy three-fingered PW signpost set in boulders inviting you to take an alternative route.

The alternative route bears left to a wall which you follow for about a mile, to **Hazel Burn**, where you turn right up a minor tarmac road to **Hareshaw House**. This unofficial alternative is quite useful when visibility is minimal, as it is easier to navigate.

Shunning the unofficial alternative, continue ahead, with the path as it contours around the side of **School Crag** in the distance on the right. A small plantation is also visible away to the right. Try and keep roughly north along the path, which does resemble a sheep track in places. You pass a circular stone sheepfold on the left, cross two tributaries of Hareshaw Burn (the first via a small bridge), passing **Callerhues Crag** on your right. Eventually you will reach a gate in a stone wall by a copse of trees, which is before, and to the right of the trees by **Hareshaw House**. Go through the small wooden gate in the wall and go right to a wooden footbridge with wooden railing on both sides. Cross this and bear left up to a wooden step stile in the wire fence, next to a wooden gate. Cross the stile (quite boggy here sometimes) and walk ahead a few yards to a tarmac road.

Turn right on the road and walk towards what looks like a large abandoned barn. The chimney on one half of the building indicates that this was once a home (**Hareshaw Cottage**) as well as a barn. Just past it, cross the wall on your left via a ladder stile (to the right of a wooden gate) and walk ahead (four-bar wooden fence on your left) to go through a wooden gate in the wall ahead (or use the wooden ladder stile on its right). Cross the enclosed field to another ladder stile on the left of a wooden gate in the wall opposite, next to a PW signpost (Public Footpath and yellow chevron pointing back and Pennine Way, Public Bridleway and blue chevron pointing ahead). Cross the stile. Immediately in front is a short guidepost to help you. Follow the blue directional arrow as you are on a bridleway, ignoring the two footpaths, which go off to the left. The grassy track you are following, used to be an old mineral railway, and it will take you to the **B6320** road. Cross the wooden ladder step stile to the left of the five-bar wooden gate and cross the road with care. There are PW signposts with solitary finger posts on both sides of the road. Go through the identical five-bar wooden gate on the other side of the road.

Section 17.2

After the gate, instead of taking the path that goes straight ahead, take the narrow green path that goes half right. This path goes to the left of a partially grass covered spoil heap and an old ruined colliery building that you can see on your right. You are heading towards the brown covered (heather) ridge. You will know you are on the right path if you see a short guidepost with a white acorn to the left of the path. The path becomes more obvious and snakes up the slope ahead. Once you reach the top of the ridge the path is on sunken peat where the PW has eroded the heather and grass on top. There are short guideposts with acorns on them to help navigation. You cross a small stream on a well-engineered bridge put there for grouse management. **Lough Shaw** passes by almost unnoticed. Two more small streams are crossed before you reach **Deer Play**. This is recognisable by a two-finger PW signpost set into a medium-sized cairn. Continue ahead on the peaty path. The short guideposts now have white strips and acorns on their tops. In wet weather, the path can be quite waterlogged. You cross another stream (**Black Sike**) via another well built stone bridge with a drainage pipe built into it.

Your next landmark is **Whitley Pike**, which is easily recognisable as it is in front of a wire fence and it has a tall guidepost set into a cairn and there is a stone marker with 'PW' carved into the stone. Cross the wire fence via a two-step wooden stile with a grab rail on the right. Do not continue ahead on an obvious path, but bear right downhill to reach a flagged path, which heads towards a road (unseen at present).

> There is a small hill (**South Padon**) along the same line of travel. Further away, to the right of the hill, is another hill with a large cairn on it. This is the huge pepper pot cairn on **Padon Hill**. The PW used to go right past this monument but it has now been diverted and passes it several hundred yards to the west.

You reach a tarmac road in front of a cattle grid. There is a PW sign-post here (yellow chevrons but no mileage or place names) next to the wooden fenced area by the cattle grid. Cross the road and continue in the same direction with a wire fence on your right. You now follow an engineered path with heather right up to it, crossing over a very small bump of a hill (**South Padon**). Ahead in the distance, **Redesdale Forest** appears.

You continue on the sandy path, passing **Padon Hill** away to the right. You next descend towards a corner of the forest ahead. Near the bottom of the dip, you cross a ladder stile in a wall that crosses the path. After rain, it can be quite boggy here. After the stile the path becomes slabbed and goes half right to join the stone wall on the right. You then continue ahead with the wall on your right. You cross a wire fence ahead and continue on a boggy path with reeds on both sides to a second fence, which you cross.

Here the forest needs to be pruned a bit as it has grown too close to the path since it was planted in the early 1980s. Drooping branches impede your path and occasionally a tree may topple over and block it. It is obvious looking at the route here that most people do end up walking briefly on the top of the wall.

You now climb up the steep slippery narrow path to another fence which crosses the path. Here the going gets easier. You can rest in the dry under the trees, but don't stand still too long or the midges may come out and bite you. You may also see a friendly robin here who has been kept well fed by fellow Pennine Wayfarers.

At the top of the hill you cross a wooden step stile in the wire fence, which crosses the path. There is a grab post on the left and an acorn and yellow directional marker beneath. The path gently slopes upwards and the wall bends to the right in a dogleg, the path following it, and you leave the trees behind for the moment. The path here is wider but very wet underfoot. All you can do it to hop onto solid grassy clumps to avoid the wettest bits. The wall disappears to be replaced by a wire fence. You are now passing **Brownrigg Head** and beside the path soon appear several stone markers with 'G H' on them. These are estate boundary stones for the old Redesdale estate of Gabriel Hall, High Sheriff of Northumberland in the early 1700s. As the fence bends left, the forest comes to meet it and for a while you walk under the trees on what can be very boggy sections of the path. We need duckboards or slabs here. Just when you feel that you can't stand it any more, a gate and PW signpost appear ahead and you step out onto a beautifully solid forest track at **Rookengate**. The signpost informs you that **Bellingham** is 9¾ miles behind you. By the side of the track is a very old green sign (I remember this being here in the 1980s) put up by The Forestry Commission saying that it welcomes Pennine Way walkers!

Section 17.3

The track through the forest to **Blakehopeburnhaugh** is now rela-tively straightforward. The forest has undergone quite a bit of felling and replanting over the years and the trees are no longer tall and oppressive. The path descends at first, and at a bend to the right there is a PW sign resembling a green hurdle, inviting walkers to go ahead, (with the trees to the left of the path), down an overgrown path which rejoins the same forest track further on. If you wish to take this path, (not many PW walkers seem to have done this judging by the lack of apparent use) please do, or you could just continue down the track. Further along the track, a second sign, this time on a notice board on top of a post, invites PW walkers to leave the main track for a second time and to go left on a grassy track, which becomes a path, then descends a slope, to rejoin the same main track but avoiding passing an old quarry.

This diversion does have some logic to it as huge logging lorries use the track, so keep an eye open for them and cover your face and eyes against the dust cloud as they pass by.

The track continues its descent until it reaches a farmstead by the name of **Blakehopeburnhaugh**, which has appeared in the Guinness Book of Records as the longest place name (18 letters) in England. Soon afterwards you cross a road bridge over the **Blakehope Burn** and pass some well-maintained public toilets on the left.

After a second road bridge (over the **River Rede**) look out for a vertical PW sign guiding you left, off the tarmac, back onto a track through the forest. This takes you to a river path (**River Rede** on your left), which you leave for a forest track at the entrance to **Cottonshopeburnfoot** camping and caravanning site. Although this has 19 letters, it used to be two words, which is why I suspect it never superseded **Blakehopeburnhaugh** as the longest place name. Go onto the bridge and left on the track until you get to a T-junction where you turn right and go down to a metal curved pedestrian bridge to the left of a ford, over the **River Rede**. Cross the bridge and continue on the track, passing the very photogenic **Byrness Church** on the right. Just before you reach the main **A68** road, there is a PW map board on the right. The PW signpost at the road informs you that you have travelled 14¾ miles since **Bellingham**.

Accommodation is limited in **Byrness**. The Byrness B&B is diagonally opposite on the right. To the left, down the road in Byrness village is the Forest View Inn. Joyce Taylor and her husband, Colin, run this. It used to be the old youth hostel, but it has been completely refurbished to a high standard. They are licensed and Joyce runs a minibus service between **Byrness** and Trows, which is reached from **Windy Gyle**, about half way between **Byrness** and **Kirk Yetholm**. This enables walkers to split the border crossing into two days and you have the advantage of a light pack on the first day. Other B&B providers in **Kirk Yetholm** and **Byrness** probably do the same, but if it is your intention to spend two days on the crossing between **Byrness** and **Kirk Yetholm** rather than do it 'in one', you should check with them before you book to see whether they provide this service.

To reach the Forest View Inn there is a track on the left, before you reach the main road, which runs parallel to the **A68** and this takes you to its location on The Green.

There is a camping barn at Barrowburn, which is reachable from **Windy Gyle**. You descend to Trows and continue along the road to reach it. You will need to have a sleeping bag and sleeping mat with you as there are no bunks, however you could have these posted up to your accommodation in **Bellingham** if you don't want to carry them all the way (but do check this out first with the accommodation provider). Barrowburn has toilets and kitchen facilities.

Walkers being picked up from **Kirk Yetholm** will be collected from Cocklawfoot as this is reachable from **Kirk Yetholm** (Trows is on the other side of the border ridge). I have tried all these options, however it is a strange feeling to have spent the last three weeks walking towards **Kirk Yetholm** and then spend your penultimate night there before finishing. Perhaps it is better to savour the moment, and see it for the first time when you finish the walk?

Section 18 – Byrness to Windy Gyle

Distance – 13 miles / 20.9 km (PW route only)
Height gained on PW route – 800 m (2,624 ft)
Height lost on PW route – 440 m (1,443 ft)

Route outline: Byrness to Byrness Hill; Ravens Knowe; Coquet Head; Chew Green; Rennies Burn; Lamb Hill Refuge Hut; Lamb Hill; Beefstand Hill; Mozie Law; Windy Gyle.

Russell's Cairn and Trig Point at Windy Gyle with the Cheviot ridge in the distance

The final stage of the PW can either be walked in one day, with a very early start, and a forced march where you will probably have little time to stop and stare at the beautiful sights along the border ridge, and it will involve a late finish. Alternatively, you can savour the journey and split it into two reasonably comfortable days. This will give you the chance of enjoying the last section rather than just putting your head down and slogging it out. I have done both and I prefer the two-day option. There is a camping barn at Barrowburn but more importantly, there are B&Bs at both **Byrness** and **Kirk Yetholm** who will book you in for two nights and pick you up about the halfway point between **Byrness** and **Kirk Yetholm**. **Byrness** picks up at Trows, on the east side of the ridge, and **Kirk Yetholm** picks up at Cocklawfoot on the west side of the ridge. This also means that you can slim down your pack for at least one of the two days, as you will be returning to the same B&B at the end of your first or second day.

Section 18.1

The exit point from **Byrness** lies along the **A68** between **St Francis' Church** and Forest View. Walk up the tarmac lane past the entrance to the Church to the **A68** where there is a PW signpost directing you left along the road. Cross the road, with care, and on the other (north) side of the road is a PW signpost with 'Pennine Way' and a white acorn on the post and a short post with Border County Ride on it, next to a thin strip of tarmac footpath. This takes you to a tarmac crescent where there is a gap in a hedge on the right with a PW signpost next to it. If you are coming from Forest View, you have to go up the tarmac crescent from the other side to see the PW signpost by the hedge.

Once you have your entry point, you go through the small wooden five-bar gate on the other side of the hedge and follow the path NE up a 170 metre (560 feet) climb through the forest, crossing three forest tracks on your way. There are short guideposts with acorns and yellow directional arrows along the route to guide you. A large block of the uppermost section of the forest, to the right of the path initially, and then on both sides of the path, was felled in 2012 giving you more daylight than your predecessors were used to. The last bit of the climb up the hill involves scrambling up a rocky outcrop to reach a wooden gate in a wire fence. This is a good viewpoint back, so take a small break here to catch your breath! The reservoir away to the right is Catcleugh. Go through the gate, and continue ahead to the top of the rise. **Byrness Hill** is close by on your right. There are the foundations of the old fire lookout post and a large cairn here.

> I hope the weather is good for you, as you will be following quite a rounded set of ridges all day. In fine weather the views are very impressive. This is one of the best walks of the whole Way, in my opinion, and also one of Tom Stephenson's favourites. If it is misty, at least you will have the border fence with you for much of the way, and plenty of slabs to guide you.

Once you leave the summit of **Byrness Hill**, the PW bends half left (very slightly west of north) on a narrow grassy path through rough countryside. The ridge arches away to the right. You head for, and go over one 'bump' ahead (**Saughy Crag**), and head for the next 'bump' (**Houx Hill**) on the horizon. There is a very reassuring sign here to guide you. Its message is not so happy as it warns you not to touch any military debris as it may explode and kill you!

> To the right of your walk today is a large military training ground used by thousands of soldiers. They use live ammunition on occasions, but rest assured, they will never fire across the line of the PW. There are also several paths off the PW, which are public rights of way which are safe to walk on.
>
> There are two sets of trees between **Byrness Hill** and **Houx Hill**. One is the huge **Byrness Plantation** (on the left), and the other is the **Hollin Burn Plantation** (on the right).

After **Houx Hill** is a third mound on the horizon (**Windy Crag**) and the PW heads towards it initially, then swings to the right of it. Once you pass it, the border fence appears on the left in the distance ahead. To the right of the path is another military sign. The PW passes the fence corner on the left. Don't cross the fence but continue with it on your left. The forest is visible on the other side of the fence, and the path is wider here. The next bump on the horizon is **Ravens Knowe**. Keep to the path with the fence away to your left. As you gain height, have a look back. In clear weather, the path is quite obvious. **Ravens Knowe** is soon reached. It has a large cairn on its top and a military sign on its left. This is a good photographic viewpoint.

Ahead on the left, in the distance, are the grubbed out remains of part of the forest. This is on **Ogre Hill**. The path continues towards it and when you descend into a dip, the ground levels and a large section of duckboards appear (or a boardwalk as the Americans would call it). This was laid down over a very boggy area in 1990. As you walk along it, look out for '1990' carved into one of the timbers. The boardwalk curves first to the left, then to the right, then ahead, with the deforested area and fence on your left. The boardwalk disappears when you go up another slope ahead. The fence and the deforested area are close by to aid navigation.

> Away to the right is a good aerial view of **Chew Green Roman Camp**. It is hard to appreciate it at ground level, but on the slopes above it you can see all the detail. Close by the Roman camp is the site of the medieval village of **Kemylpethe** although there are no visible remains to be seen.

The path descends again, passing a wooden step stile next to a wooden gate in the fence, by a signpost (**not** a PW signpost) and a sign 'No Vehicle Access'. Do not go left here but continue ahead, past another stile with a signpost indicating a permissive path on the left to 'The Heart's Toe'. Continue northwards, with the fence on your left, and you soon reach a dip where there is a short section of duckboards in front of a wooden gate in the corner of the wire fence.

A PW signpost (**Byrness** 3¾; **Chew Green** 1) is next to a short section of wooden fencing on the left, and a MoD sign on the right. This is a momentous moment because as you go through the gate, you are entering Scotland for the first time!

Section 18.2

Continue ahead up the slope on the other side. When the fence bends left, the PW bears right. After a short distance you come to another PW signpost (**Byrness** 4; Pennine Way Alternative Route **Windy Gyle** 8; Pennine Way **Windy Gyle** 8½).

I have taken the alternative route and, although the main route is reputed to be ½ mile longer, the navigation on the main route is easier and you get to see **Chew Green** close up. The alternative route (probably to reduce the numbers passing close to **Chew Green**) gains height as it ascends **Chew Edge** before bearing right, passing above **Chew Green**, passing **Brownhart Law** and rejoining the PW at **Dere Street**. The choice is yours.

The main route continues ahead at the signpost. In the valley below on your right is the **River Coquet**, although it is little more than a boggy ditch at present. The PW is on a wide grassy path. There are a couple of small guideposts here next to the path. As you approach the second guidepost (blue directional arrow), a new wooden gate in a wire fence should be visible in a shallow dip ahead. When you get there, cross the wooden step stile with a grab post, on the right of the gate, (welcome back to England) and continue ahead to the post on the near skyline. You shortly reach a four-finger PW signpost ('Coquet Valley' ahead; 'Restricted Byway **Dere Street**' to the right; and 'Pennine Way Restricted Byway Dere Street' to the left, [the old three-finger signpost pointing left here used to say **Lamb Hill** 3]; and 'Pennine Way Public Bridleway **Byrness** 4¾' pointing back the way you have just walked). Turn left here and go up the slope, with the **Chew Green Roman Camp** on your left.

You will pass an interesting sign here indicating an archaeological area with no digging or vehicles allowed, but soldiers are allowed in the area, judging by the diagrams on it. If you look back down the slope you will see a tarmac road on the other side of the **River Coquet**. This is the road that links **Byrness** with Trows and Barrowburn.

Section 18.3

Climb up the slope to the top of the camp, to reach a guidepost (plum coloured directional arrow indicating a Restricted Byway) where you turn right, down a slope to a wooden footbridge over **Chew Sike**. The path down to the bridge and up the other side is mostly slabbed. The bridge has ramps either side, which is unusual. The PW ascends the slope (on **Dere Street** which is a Roman Road linking York with Scotland) and passes a small tatty old fenced enclosure on the left before passing below **Brownhart Law** also on the left, on a worn narrow path.

Brownhart Law had a Roman Signal Station (on the other side of the fence) which is clearly visible on aerial photographs.

After a short distance you reach a PW signpost with plum chevrons (**Chew Green** ¼ behind; public footpath to Makendon 1 mile to the right; **Lamb Hill** 2¾ miles ahead). Some yards further up the slope you come to a metal gate in a fence, which crosses the path. Go through the little wooden gate to the right of the metal gate (acorn on the right gate post), and continue on the ascending grassy track. At a PW signpost (plum chevrons – **Chew Green** ½ mile behind; **Lamb Hill** 2½ miles ahead; Bridleway to Deel's Hill 1 mile and Blindburn 2¾ miles to the right), the PW alternative route (footpath) rejoins the PW main route. You continue ahead through a small wooden gate in a (part wooden) fence and cut across a corner of the border and briefly re-enter Scotland. There is no exit gate but the border fence is again on your left. The PW is a wide green level path here.

Your next landmark is a fence corner where there is a green metal sign on a wooden gate near the corner. The sign says that this is a section of **Dere Street** from Towford to the border and that it is a scheduled ancient monument. On the fence corner used to be a rather ancient moss covered four-finger PW signpost, which, like many others, was replaced sometime during 2010 / 2011. The PW ahead is a Public Bridleway (blue chevron; **Lamb Hill** 2) and **Chew Green** (plum chevron) is 1 mile behind. The other two finger posts point to **Dere Street**, half left (Towford 3) and a Public Bridleway half right (Blindburn 3). The PW leaves **Dere Street** at this point and continues ahead on a grassy path with the wire border fence going away on your left.

You are now about to cut off a corner in the border fence. The path has the occasional short guidepost with a white acorn and directional arrow to help navigation.

You initially head north, cross a small stream (**Buckham's Walls Burn**), and at a cairn on the left of the path bear right (NE), passing another guidepost. You then descend into the first feeder stream of **Rennies Burn** (guidepost), after which you descend down a steep bank into **Rennies Burn** proper and ascend up the slope on the other side to more level ground, passing another guidepost where you soon meet the border fence once again.

In 2013, Natural England provided £160,000 to the Northumberland National Parks Authority to replace the boardwalk at **Auchope Cairn**. It also funded 60 metres of recycled sandstone flags at **Wedder Hill**, which is the area you have just walked across. These were to replace existing flagstones, which had sunk into the peat, sometimes up to a boot's height. This isn't usually a problem in warm dry summer weather, but it is no fun when they are under water, and there have been a couple of very wet winters recently which haven't helped matters much. Me? I usually carry a stick and I can test the ground in front of me to see if there is an actual slab there or a gap. This goes back to when I walked the Pennine Way in the late 1970s when you really did need a probe to see just how firm the ground was in front of you. When you were carrying a heavy pack you did not want to sink into the peat!

The blanket bog, which covers the Cheviots, provides a habitat for numerous plants and wildlife, including wild goats (often seen by PW walkers). The National Park Authority needs to keep walkers on the slabs and not step off them to avoid sunken slabs, causing more erosion and damage to this fragile environment.

At the fence corner, turn left, with the fence. Ahead, what looks like a wooden bus shelter is in fact the **Yearning Saddle Mountain Refuge Hut** (OS grid reference NT 804 128). The hill half right ahead is **Lamb Hill**. Leave the fence and descend to the hut. Inside it is small but cosy.

If the weather is particularly bad, walkers have spent the night here. If you are forced to make an unplanned overnight stop, try and ring your intended overnight on your mobile phone to let them know. There is a narrow bench around the inside (too narrow to sleep on) and a visitor's book, which may keep you entertained while you are there. It is a good place for a break out of the wind / sun / rain. There is a small brass plaque on the inside wall celebrating the life of John Weatherall (1927 – 2008) who was a founder member and former President of the Pennine Way Association. In life, John was a great man, both mentally and physically. He had his roots in the PW and was involved in its creation on the ground when he worked in the Northumberland National Park & Countryside Department as a Rights of Way Officer. Many a work party on the Pennine Way had John leading it or helping out.

Section 18.4

Leave the hut and turn left up the obvious path up **Lamb Hill**, with the border fence on your left. On a clear day, if you look back, you can see the path both to and from the refuge hut. Near the top of the hill, slabs appear underfoot.

Here I don't complain about slabs as I clearly remember the 1970s and 1980s without slabs and duckboards when the border ridge was a place of dread in wet weather as it was extremely boggy in places underfoot. I sometimes had to resort to shuffling sideways along the wire strands of the border fence itself to avoid having to make a long detour away from the fence to try and find a reasonably dry patch on which to continue the walk. This involved constant jumping over the shorter boggy sections. If you miscalculated, you went into the bog up to your waist. A walking stick was essential to test the ground in front of you to see if it would take your weight. Either way, you zigzagged along the PW looking for firm ground, adding miles to walk. I used to walk this section in the spring, as the frozen peat was easier to walk on.

On the summit of **Lamb Hill**, on the Scottish side of the fence, is a trig point (S 7989). It may look a bit forlorn, as it isn't usually as well painted as its southern cousins. Continue ahead on the slabs. A few minutes later you will see a reminder of how wet it can be on the top when you cross a wooden pallet-like footbridge over one of the boggy bits. The slabs and bridge keep your boots dry. Several yards later, you cross a second pallet-like footbridge. **Beefstand Hill** is the next summit, although there is little to mark its passing. Continue along the slabbed path with the border fence on your left. After **Beefstand Hill** and just before **Mozie Law** you come to a metal gate in a wire fence, and cross over a wooden ladder stile to the right of it.

Further along the PW you may find that in at least one place, the slabs have sunk a bit and are under water. They are still there. This is where your stick comes in handy. It will confirm (or deny) that the way ahead is safe to place your foot.

The next 'highlight' is a corner in the slabbed path as it follows a corner in the fence. Well worth a photograph! From here, you can see the PW going on in the distance. The slabs and the lighter green on either side are a contrast to the brown heather on the ridge. Soon afterwards at a tall guidepost with an acorn on it, (which you reach shortly after passing a metal gate on the left), you will see ahead, half right in the distance, the ridge you will soon be walking on.

Looking ahead the PW goes over one 'bump' with the delightful name of **Foul Step**. The second, higher hill, to the right of it, with a large cairn, is **Windy Gyle**. The cairn on the top is huge and even has its own name – **Russell's Cairn**.

After the tall guidepost, the path, which initially looks like a vehicle track, parallels the fence for a while and descends downhill for a short distance, before it becomes slabbed again, at which point it bears right, away from the border fence, towards the first 'bump'.

The path descends (no slabs) towards a dip where it meets a wooden gate (with 'shut the gate' on a rectangular yellow sign) and a wooden step stile on the left. This is **Plea Knowe**. There is a four-finger PW signpost here (**Mozie Law** ½ behind on the bridleway; **Windy Gyle** 1½ ahead).

A Roman Road called '**The Street**' crosses the PW here. On the right is an exit point to the Coquet Valley, but don't use this as there is a much better one further on if you are intending to go that way for your pick up back to **Byrness**.

Note: In Autumn 2011 there was an extinguishment order here, which extinguished the line of the PW along the line of The Street. After Autumn 2011 the PW no longer continued ahead on the fence for a short distance at this point, before it curved NEE to meet a look-alike border fence (the actual Border fence is out of sight to the north).

Instead the PW now immediately bears half right (NE) for 375 yards, away from the border fence and curves roughly eastwards for 275 yards to meet a look-alike border fence at a corner by a star marker. I suspect that the revised path follows the line of an existing footpath, which was used by PW walkers up to that point in time, so that most walkers wouldn't have known any difference anyway.

The PW heads down a grassy path towards a deep gully. This is the upper end of **Foulstep Sike**. You should be able to clearly see the brown scar of the path climbing half right out of it to meet a newly refurbished section of fence at a corner. There is a six-pointed metal star marker here on a metal post. You may have seen a similar one at **Chew Green**. Once you meet the fence, continue ahead with the fence on your left. The path then skirts the right side of a hill ahead of you, moving away from the fence with a valley with **Rowhope Burn** flowing through it on your right. The path along the ridge ahead, with a new section of fence on your left, is clearly visible, with **Russell's Cairn** in the distance, slightly to the left of the path. The PW dips onto a saddle on the ridge, meeting the fence once again, and then climbs up the other side. Just before the dip, there is another good view of **Russell's Cairn** and in good visibility you can see the PW signpost to the right of it. On the way up the hill is a five-bar wooden gate. There is an acorn and a blue directional arrow on the right gatepost. If you go through the gate (into Scotland) this will cut off a corner of the fence and take you to the summit of **Windy Gyle**. This is the official PW. You can of course pass the gate and continue up the slope with the fence on your left and cross the fence via the wooden step stile further up on the summit, closer to the cairn. **Russell's Cairn** is a Bronze Age mound and very impressive. A trig point (S 7999) is built into the cairn (see photograph at the start of this section).

Windy Gyle to Trows

It is vitally important that you have the correct OS maps with you for the route down to Trows if you are being picked up there for a second night in your accommodation in Byrness, or walking to Barrowburn which is about 1¼ miles further on. There is little signage to help you once you leave the PW. The PW signpost (**Chew Green** 7¼; **The Schil** 7) by **Russell's Cairn** helpfully has a third finger post pointing SSE to the Coquet Valley, 2¾ miles away. Trows is a little further along this valley.

From **Russell's Cairn**, walk to the border fence on the slabbed path and cross the wooden step stile to the left of a four-bar wooden gate. Continue in the same direction, down the slope on a grassy path. Just before Scotchman's Ford, the path forks. There is a short guidepost here. Take the right fork, down a grassy track towards a forested area ahead. The track passes to the right of this plantation. At a second fork, keep right, to a wall. Go through the gate, and keep on the grassy track to a second metal gate. There is a yellow sign on the other side of the gate, which says that the green track you have walked down is 'out of bounds to military vehicles'. Continue ahead in the same direction down to a narrow tarmac road and cross Trows Burn, just before the road, using a wooden footbridge on the right. Pass the stone barn and Trows is the drab two-storey muddy brown building on a hill by the side of the road. Getting to Trows involves losing about 330 metres (1,083 feet) in height from **Russell's Cairn** and you will need to regain that height again in the morning.

Section 19 – Windy Gyle to Kirk Yetholm

Distance (High Level) – 15.3 miles / 24.6 km
Distance (Low Level) – 14.9 miles / 24.1 km
Height gained on PW route (High Level) – 765 m (2,509 ft)
Height lost on PW route (High Level) – 1,150 m (3,773 ft)
Height gained on PW route (Low Level) – 655 m (2,148 ft)
Height lost on PW route (Low Level) – 1,145 m (3,756 ft)
(All above distances and heights include The Cheviot)

Route outline: Windy Gyle to Clennell Street; King's Seat; Score Head; Cairn Hill (West Top); The Cheviot; Cairn Hill (West Top); Auchope Cairn; Auchope Mountain Refuge Hut; The Schil; **High Level route** – White Law; Whitelaw Nick; Halter Burn; Kirk Yetholm; **Low Level route** – Old Halterburnhead (ruin); Halterburnhead Farm (Burnhead); Halter Burn, Kirk Yetholm.

Cairn Hill (West Top) – boardwalk now replaced by slabs

Section 19.1

From **Russell's Cairn** on **Windy Gyle**, the PW continues in the same direction that you approached the cairn (from the wooden gate you went through) yesterday, i.e. ENE. The finger post on the PW sign-post (**The Schil** 7) will guide you. The other two finger posts inform you that **Chew Green** is 7¼ miles behind you and the Coquet Valley is 2¾ miles on the right. Basically the cairn is on your left and the border fence is on the right. The section between the signpost and the exit stile doesn't have any slabs.

> If you really are unsure about where to go, and want a blindingly obvious way to rejoin the PW, at the signpost by **Russell's Cairn**, just follow the Coquet Valley line of slabs to the border fence, cross it at the wooden step stile and turn left, so that the border fence is on your left. The path is slabbed so just follow it until you meet the exit stile on the border fence, (don't cross the stile as you want to remain on the English side).

The PW descends from the **Windy Gyle** summit. Ahead on the skyline is the broad summit of **Cairn Hill**, and along the connecting ridge to the right, is **The Cheviot**. About half a mile from **Windy Gyle**, and 50 metres (160 feet) below it, you pass, to the right of a second large cairn (tumulus) with a six-star metal marker on it, indicating that it too is a site of antiquity. Just before you get to the cairn, the slabs underfoot change from a single line to a double line for a brief period. There is a fence with a gate in it on the Scottish side just before the cairn (don't go through it).

You continue down the slope, still with the border fence on your left, but without slabs underfoot. It is almost as if they ran out and then they were doubled up by the cairn to get rid of them before the slope started again! The PW descends again and when the terrain levels out a bit, the slabs return. A short time after, you cross a wooden step stile in a wire fence ahead (acorn and yellow directional arrow on the fence post on the left of the stile) and the slabs turn left for a few feet to a wooden gate, then right again as you continue with the border fence on your left (again don't go through the gate).

Soon after, the slabs pass a slight bend in the border fence and on the corner post surprisingly, is a road traffic sign! It is the one where there is a motorcyclist passing over the top of a car, with '1st April to 31st May except for access' below it. Some yards ahead is a large five-bar wooden gate on the left and a PW signpost on the right. The slabs stop here for a while. Two of the finger posts indicate that **Chew Green** is now 8½ miles behind you and **The Schil** is 6 miles ahead. The other two finger posts inform you that you are standing on **Clennell Street**, an important Roman Road. To the left, through the gate is Cocklawfoot, 2½ miles away. To the right is a Restricted Byway to Alwinton, 9 miles away.

Clennell Street to Cocklawfoot

If you need to get to Cocklawfoot to pick up your transport into **Kirk Yetholm**, **Clennell Street** is where you should leave the PW.

It is vitally important that you have the correct OS maps with you for the route down to Cocklawfoot as there is little signage to help you once you leave the PW.

When you arrive at the PW signpost with four finger posts, (one pointing left saying Clennell Street Cocklawfoot 2½), you go through the gate in the border fence on the left, past the traffic sign (on the right) initially following a wire fence on your left. The wide green track is very obvious and initially heads NNW down the slope of Outer Cock Law where it curves right around some earthworks, levels off for a while as it approaches Cock Law, then curves right at Camp Tops, then curves left and enters a short, but wide plantation. When it emerges out of the trees it follows a wall on the right, past another small plantation on the right, before reaching the farmstead of Cocklawfoot.

Accommodation on or near the border ridge is virtually non-existent. There used to be a B&B at Uswayford, 1½ miles SE of the border fence, for many years, but farming and indeed living in the borders in winter can be hard. An example of this is Trows B&B, which was intended to plug the gap left by Uswayford, but Trows itself is now abandoned. Only Barrowburn is left in terms of accommodation within walking distance of the border ridge (see section 18 for details).

Section 19.2

At the signpost on **Clennell Street**, go past the gate in the border fence on the left and continue ahead with the border fence still on your left. The flagstone path is quite close to the fence here. If you look back, **Russell's Cairn** is still quite visible on the horizon. After about 5–6 minutes of walking you come across another corner in the flags. This time the corner forms three steps down to the right, away from the fence, before they angle left again back to the fence and continue ahead as usual.

These little anomalies are quite helpful in what could otherwise be a bland section of slabs. Occasionally you see a reminder just how wet the border ridge can get. The slabs are such an improvement on floundering in the bogs.

There is the occasional bend in the fence and you have to cross a short ladder stile over a three-bar wooden fence, which cuts across the PW, but you will, after about 30 minutes from **Clennell Street**, arrive at **King's Seat**, which has an unpainted trig point (S 7997) just over the border fence. It is a long slog from here to **Cairn Hill (West Top)** but it is difficult to get lost because it is slabbed and you always have the border fence on your left.

There are the occasional new(ish) slabs, noticeable because they are a different shape, and sometimes a different colour from the ones originally laid in the path. There are also the occasional stunted guideposts with acorns on them. These must date back to before the slabs went in as they are right by the slabbed route. These are about as useful as an ashtray on a motorbike.

Not too far below **Cairn Hill (West Top)** is a wooden gate in the border fence. It is worth taking a breather here for two reasons. The first is that on a clear sunny day there is a good view, a few feet to the right of the gate over the fence, of the summit cairn of **The Schil**. The second is that if you follow the ridgeline back, you will see a white square on the second hill before **The Schil**. This is **Auchope Mountain Refuge Hut** (OS grid reference NT 877201) near **Red Cribs**. This is one of the reasons why I think it is better to split the final day into two, as you would miss so much otherwise.

Just before you get to the top of the slope up to **Cairn Hill (West Top)**, look for a large rock on the right, next to the path. Bearing in mind the terrain you have walked over, this is unusual in itself, but this rock has a plaque on it ('In memory of Stan Hudson Died 12 July 1981'). Shortly after this, the slabs stop and a boardwalk section begins, and about five minutes later you arrive at **Cairn Hill (West Top)**. It is hard to believe that the National Park Voluntary Warden Service installed this section of boardwalk during July and August 1989. It is still in remarkably good condition. There is a three-fingered PW signpost here. **Windy Gyle** is now 4 miles behind you. **The Schil** is 3 miles to your left (over the stile in the four-bar wooden fence), and **The Cheviot** is 1¼ miles half right, over the stile in the wire fence, along the slabs. If you are taking two days, and the weather is favourable, you will have time to walk the 2½ miles to **The Cheviot** summit and back (1¼ miles each way). If you do, you will return to **Cairn Hill (West Top)**, where you are now.

Section 19.3
Cairn Hill (West Top) to The Cheviot

Cross the wooden step stile over the wire fence on the right and head slightly north of east on the slabbed path. Don't get too complacent as there is a section of the path, (approximately 675 yards – which has to be walked both ways!), where the slabs stop for some reason. It is quite boggy on that section without them. You really appreciate them when they are gone! The slabbed path goes gradually up the slope in front of you. There is a PW signpost ¾ mile from the summit, just before you get to **Cairn Hill**, where a path goes off to the right to the Harthope Valley. The PW continues up the slope and, at **Cairn Hill,** goes NE. It is just before you reach the signpost that the slabs disappear. The signpost itself is in the middle of a wet, boggy, grassless peat bog. A bit like **Black Hill** used to be before it was tamed with slabs and re-vegetated. Keep to the far left of the signpost where there is firmer ground. Hopefully one day this section will be slabbed too.

The slabs reappear! You should have a wire fence on your right. All is well with the world once again! Occasionally a slab is laid sideways so that it can act as a passing place. About half an hour after leaving the guidepost, you cross a wire fence corner by means of two stiles – a wooden step stile with grab handle on the left (acorn and yellow directional marker on the crossbar above the stile) going into the fenced area, and a second (to the left of a wooden gate) as you exit it. A few yards beyond the fence corner is a trig point (S 1560), perched on top of a very tall concrete platform, which marks the summit.

> In good weather, it should take you about 60 to 90 minutes to get to **The Cheviot** and back. It is, despite what some guide-books may say, part of the PW and it is an interesting walk. If Wainwright can walk it, so can you!

Section 19.4

Back at **Cairn Hill (West Top)**, you go through the wooden gate in the four-bar wooden fence and head NW on a recently laid (2013) slabbed section of the path to **Auchope Cairn**. This is a pepper pot shaped cairn on the right of the path.

Prior to spring 2013, you would have continued ahead on a boardwalk, which was installed during July and August 1989 by the National Park Voluntary Warden Service, as the boardwalk made a beeline towards **Auchope Cairn**. However in early 2013, this 1,000 metre section of boardwalk was replaced by hundreds of tons of flagstones airlifted onto the Border Ridge, and levered into place by local contractors. Like all things, boardwalks have a finite life and this section was beginning to sink into the peat on one side, making it a bit like a fairground roller coaster ride, hence the need for action.

Once again the PW leaves the top to travel down a broad ridge towards the next objective. There is quite a steep descent (approximately 240 metres / 800 feet) down the grassy slope. The border fence is still on your left but several yards away. Once you reach the dip, you now have to gain some height again to reach the **Auchope Mountain Refuge Hut** on the horizon ahead of you. From the bottom of the slope it looks like a small wooden matchbox. The path up the slope is quite grassy so it doesn't take too long. Once there, it is a good spot for a break out of the weather.

The current shelter, which was flown onto the site by helicopter in 1988, replaced an earlier one, put there about 1971. The earlier shelter was an old railway goods wagon, complete with sliding door (see photograph at end of the *History of the Pennine Way* section), which had a habit of jamming in freezing weather so you left it open! It had to be replaced when it began to fall apart. The timber was removed and burnt *in situ* and the metal work removed when conditions became favourable. The current shelter was initially erected on the lawn of the Head Warden at Brandon, and then airlifted piece-meal by 202 Squadron RAF Boulmer. An all terrain vehicle came up to the border ridge from Mounthooly in the College Valley carrying the remaining materials. The Northumberland National Parks Wardens, Voluntary Wardens and Fell Rescue Team, along with John Weatherall (Rights of Way Officer for the Northumberland National Park & Countryside Department), were all involved. The new shelter was moved approximately ten metres into Northumberland, on the English side of the border fence, so it is now under the jurisdiction of the Northumberland National Park. It is taller at the front than the back and very well made, with duckboards along the front and seating all the way round the outside. There is a brass plaque inside the shelter informing visitors about the erection of the replacement shelter. Again, there is a visitor's book in a slot in the wooden interior walls and there are benches all around the inside.

From the shelter, you can clearly see your next objective, which is **The Schil**, along a broad ridge, which curves to the right. The rocky outcrop on the summit is clearly visible in good weather.

Exit the hut, turning left on a reasonably level grassy path. The fence is faithfully on your left. After a short while it bends to the left and you pass **Red Cribs** on the right. There is a path here, which descends into the valley to Mounthooly Bunkhouse, about 1½ miles NE. Just before the final bump before **The Schil**, there are a section of slabs over a particularly boggy part of the path. On the final corner in the fence before **The Schil**, there is a stubby guidepost with a white acorn on it. At first, the path is only slightly sloped but it can be muddy in wet weather. There is another section of slabs here just before you reach a wooden step stile with a grab handle, in a four-bar wooden fence that crosses the path. There is an acorn and a yellow directional arrow on the top bar. It is very boggy on both sides of the stile. Now the slope increases as you climb an obvious path a few yards away from the fence. Nearer the top, the path goes right up to the fence and becomes narrower but grassier and a bit rocky underfoot. On the summit, there are several rocky outcrops that are very photogenic.

> You might be lucky enough to see a snow bunting here on the fence. The more distinctive male is about the size of a sparrow and has a pinkish-brown breast.

If you are considering taking the Low Level alternative into **Kirk Yetholm**, this is your last climb of the day. If you have the time and energy, I strongly recommend that you take the High Level route as it is much prettier and actually not that much harder.

Again, descend down the obvious grassy path NW down towards a col ahead of you. If the weather is kind you will be able to see, that ahead of you, the border fence changes to a wall. You reach the wall corner on your left. The wall, which now runs parallel with the PW, is broken so there is an additional wire fence (between you and the wall) to keep in any livestock etc. After a short while, next to a metal gate, you cross a wooden step stile (acorn and directional arrow but broken grab bar) in a wire fence that crosses the path. Not long afterwards you descend to a PW signpost by a ladder stile, next to a wooden gate in the wall. This informs you that **Windy Gyle** is now 7¾ miles behind you (the old signpost used to tell you that **The Schil** was 1 mile behind). **Kirk Yetholm** (yes the finish point is finally mentioned!) is 4½ miles left over the ladder stile. Another finger post points to Mounthooly Bunkhouse 1¾ miles in the opposite direction to **Kirk Yetholm**.

Cross the stile, leaving England for the very last time. The rest of the PW now lies in Scotland. Head roughly WNW on an obvious path away from the wall. The path becomes a grassy track and you pass a short PW guidepost on the right of the track with a painted acorn and arrow, as you go up the slope. Soon you reach a PW signpost where it is decision time. **Windy Gyle** is now 8¼ miles behind but there is a junction here where you need to choose between the Low Level 'alternative route' (4 miles) and the High Level 'main route' (4½ miles).

Note: You were 4½ miles from **Kirk Yetholm** according to the earlier signpost when you crossed the ladder stile over the wall.

The obvious choice is the lower shorter route but don't be hasty! Half a mile isn't too much if you are not feeling too tired and you have sufficient time left. On the High Level route you stay on the fells with all those lovely views to keep the spirit uplifted! However, if you are doing the border ridge in one day, you will probably have had enough and all you want to do is finish and have your free half pint in the **Border Hotel**, followed by a nice meal and a shower. Don't worry, I understand!

Corbie Craig (junction of High / Low alternative routes)

High Level route from Corbie Craig to Kirk Yetholm

Section 19.5

The High Level route was originally suggested to the Countryside Commission for Scotland by the Pennine Way Council (now the Pennine Way Association) who have adopted it as the main route.

The High Level route forks to the right at the signpost and goes up a grassy track to a small wooden gate. Just before is another short PW guidepost on the left of the track with a painted acorn and arrow. Go through the gate and (surprisingly for a high level route) go downhill along **Steer Rig** with a wire fence (the border fence) on your right.

Be very careful of the rusty top strand of barbed wire. The views ahead are very impressive. As you descend the slope, look to the left ahead for a group of trees in the valley below. This is the ruined **Old Halterburnhead,** which is on the Low Level route. Either because most people use the Low Level route, or because the High Level route is newer, there is a very good springy grassy track on this section.

The occasional white acorn appears on fence posts on the right. In the col is a small wooden gate (by a larger metal gate) in the fence on your right (ignore this). Now begins the climb up the slope to **White Law**. This is the only real uphill on this section and it is again on a good grassy path. Take a couple of breathing stops to admire the views and to shoot a few photographs of the rolling hills on either side.

At **White Law**, descend WNW down the clear grassy path to a ladder stile by a stone wall corner at **Whitelaw Nick**. There is a PW signpost here directing you to cross the ladder stile and descend northwards down the slope, with a wall on your right, to reach **Stob Rig**. The path undulates (you are in Scotland). At **Stob Rig** you leave the wall (which continues ahead), and you continue on a well-defined path, which contours half left up a slope to a short PW guidepost with a painted acorn. A few minutes later you come to a PW signpost. **Windy Gyle** is now 10½ miles behind and you are only 2 miles from **Kirk Yetholm**. The third finger post points towards Trowhopeburn (or Trowupburn on the OS map) 1½ miles away. At the signpost you bear left on a good wide grassy track that winds its way down the hillside. Ahead can be seen a tarmac road which leads to **Kirk Yetholm**. The large bump ahead with the earthworks around the top is Green Humbleton hill. The earthworks are the remains of an old Iron Age fort. The PW passes to the left of the hill. You shortly reach another PW signpost, which tells you that **White Law** is 1 mile behind, and **Kirk Yetholm** is now only 1¾ miles ahead with Elsdonburn 1½ miles away via St Cuthbert's Way on the right (although the finger post doesn't have an apostrophe). St Cuthbert's Way and the Pennine Way share the same footpath into **Kirk Yetholm**.

Continue down the wide grassy track towards a small plantation below a hill ahead. You will next come to a fork in the track just before a corrugated iron shed on the left. Ignore the path to the left and continue ahead, passing a plastic St Cuthbert's Way sign on a short guidepost set in a small cairn on the right of the path. Pass the shed on the left and continue down the slope towards the plantation. The track narrows to a sandy path as it contours through the ferns, high above **Shielknowe Burn**, around Green Humbleton hill. You pass a second St Cuthbert's Way sign on a short guidepost. This one also has a directional arrow and a white acorn. The road at **Halter Burn** is clearly visible on the right. Walk ahead to the stone wall, and follow it down to the burn which you cross and walk ahead to the tarmac road. There is a joint PW and St Cuthbert's Way signpost here.

You will also notice an E2 sign surrounded by a circle of stars on the post. This relates to the fact that you are also on the European Long Distance Footpath E2, which runs from Stranraer to Nice, which was officially opened on 15 September 1999.

Turn right on the road, crossing a cattle grid. The road unfortunately now goes over a small hill and there is a second hill before you reach **Kirk Yetholm**. However the last stretch is on tarmac and technically you shouldn't go wrong. About 20–30 minutes after reaching the road you should be in **Kirk Yetholm**. The last PW map board is on the village green. A slightly more interesting map board is on the wooden bus shelter on the left of the green. This is a copy of one of the 24 original map boards, which were placed on the PW many decades ago. The original locations of the other 23 are shown on this map board but don't expect to see them, as they are long gone.

Congratulations, you have walked the Pennine Way!

Please take a moment to read the final notes at the end of the Low Level route section below, as these contains some useful information about transport from Kirk Yetholm.

Low Level route from Corbie Craig to Kirk Yetholm

Section 19.6

Instead of taking the right fork at the signpost, bear left on the Low Level alternative path (**Kirk Yetholm** 4 miles) which curves round to the left on a gradual sloping grassy track. Go through a small five-bar wooden gate, next to a larger wooden gate in a wire fence, which crosses the path. The PW continues its descent approximately NNW around the hillside on a path that is sometimes used by cattle, judging by the deposits on or around the path. The ruin of **Old Halterburnhead** in a small copse of trees appears ahead. The path becomes less green and approaches a wall ahead. Just before it reaches the wall there is a plain PW signpost.

Continue on the descending path to another five-bar gate next to a larger wooden gate in an old crumbling dry stone wall (with a secondary wire fence next to it) and go through it. There is a short guidepost, with a yellow directional arrow and painted white acorn, a few yards beyond the gate. Follow the directional arrow and continue on a gradual descent, initially in the same direction, but later you curve to the right, down the slope, on a good path through bracken to reach an old low wall corner (with a wire fence inside it to control livestock) just before **Old Halterburnhead**. There is another short guidepost here.

Continue ahead, with the wall on your left, past the ruins and trees to another PW signpost. Bear left on a track, which crosses **Latchly Sike** as it curves round to the left. On the hillside opposite is an old National Carriers wagon, which is being used as an animal shelter. Further along is a circular sheepfold on the right. The green track goes over a rise. Just before you reach some farm buildings ahead on the left (**Burnhead** on OS maps), a PW signpost diverts you right, down to an impressive wooden footbridge over a stream. A guidepost with a painted acorn on it keeps you on the right line to the footbridge.

Cross the footbridge and turn left, up to a wooden kissing gate in the corner of a wall, with a PW signpost next to it. Go through the gate and continue ahead with the wall immediately on your left. The slope on the right comes down close to the path leaving a narrow passage between it and the wall. This will bring you out past the farm buildings you saw from the path.

The old PW used to go right through the farm (as it was then) but it has since changed usage and it is now a horse breeding and riding stables and it has changed its name to **Halterburnhead Farm**. This is probably what caused the diversion too.

The dry stone wall changes into a wire fence, and when you are opposite the horse paddock there is a small five-bar gate, a very grand step stile with railings, and a PW signpost. Go through the gate and bear half right down the taped off (for horses) grassy bank to the road. You follow this road, first NW then NNW, over a cattle grid and past a substantial dwelling amongst some pine trees on the left, and continue to a second cattle grid where the High Level route meets it at **Halter Burn**. There is a joint PW and St Cuthbert's Way signpost here.

You will also notice an E2 sign surrounded by a circle of stars on the post. This relates to the fact that you are also on the European Long Distance Footpath E2, which runs from Stranraer to Nice, which was officially opened on 15 September 1999.

Continue ahead on the road, crossing a cattle grid. The road unfortunately now goes over a small hill and there is a second hill before you reach **Kirk Yetholm**. However the last stretch is on tarmac and technically you shouldn't go wrong. About 20–30 minutes after reaching the road you should be in **Kirk Yetholm**. The last PW map board is on the village green. A slightly more interesting map board is on the wooden bus shelter on the left of the green. This is a copy of one of the 24 original map boards, which were placed on the PW many decades ago. The original locations of the other 23 are shown on this map board but don't expect to see them, as they are long gone.

Congratulations, you have walked the Pennine Way!

Please take a moment to read the final notes below, as these contains some useful information about transport from Kirk Yetholm.

And finally...

A word of caution about your arrival day in **Kirk Yetholm**!

The bus to Kelso does not run on a Sunday, so unless you want to get a taxi there, try and arrange your arrival day for any day except Saturday (unless you have private transport arranged). There are buses running from Kelso on a Sunday but these are obviously less frequent. Secondly, if you are travelling from Kelso to Berwick-upon-Tweed (to pick up a train), there is only a 5-minute gap between the early bus and your connection at Kelso. Do take this into account and spend some quality time in Kelso where you will find an interesting ruined abbey and shops to keep you occupied while you wait for the next bus.

The Website addresses for the two bus companies involved are:
Munro's of Jedburgh (Service 81) Kirk Yetholm to Kelso:
http://www.munrosofjedburgh.co.uk

Perryman's Buses (Service 67) Kelso to Berwick-upon-Tweed railway station: *http://www.perrymansbuses.co.uk*

I hope you enjoyed it enough to want to come back and do it again sometime (or at least your favourite bits).

If you would like to write an article for the Pennine Way Association's biannual newsletter, the contact point for their Newsletter Editor can be found on their website at *http://www.penninewayassociation. co.uk*

Mileage and height gained table: South to North

The table below is intended to help you with your planning. As this book is written for walkers starting at Edale and walking to Kirk Yetholm, Edale is at the top. Those of you with sharp eyes will have noticed that the total distance isn't the official guide's 268 miles. That figure includes all the alternatives and most walkers will not walk all of these on their trip. The distances below have been carefully measured on the OS maps and what you see is what you get.

Start Point	Distance km	Distance miles	Total km	Total miles	Height gained metres	Height gained feet
Edale	0.0	0.0			0	0
Kinder Downfall	8.0	5.0			490	1,608
Snake Pass (A57)	7.0	4.3			100	328
Crowden (turn off)	11.0	6.8	**26.0**	**16.1**	200	656
Black Hill	7.0	4.3			440	1,444
Wessenden Head (A635)	2.8	1.7			60	197
Blakely Clough (GR054090)	3.8	2.3			10	33
Standedge (A62)	4.3	2.6	**17.9**	**10.9**	160	525
A640 (Haigh Gutter)	3.5	2.2			90	295
M62	3.6	2.2			80	262
A58 (White House)	4.0	2.5			110	361
Withens Gate	7.2	4.5	**18.3**	**11.4**	40	131
A646 (Calderdale)	5.5	3.4			40	131
Gorple Cottages	6.8	4.2			410	1,345

Start Point	Distance km	Distance miles	Total km	Total miles	Height gained metres	Height gained feet
Ponden Reservoir	10.0	6.2	**22.3**	**13.9**	235	771
A6068 (Ickornshaw)	8.8	5.5			265	869
Lothersdale (road)	4.0	2.5			185	607
Brown House Farm	6.0	3.7	**18.8**	**11.7**	205	673
A59 (East Marton)	3.6	2.2			75	246
Gargrave (A65)	4.2	2.6			30	98
Airton	6.1	3.8			110	361
Malham	4.0	2.5	**17.9**	**11.1**	90	295
Malham Cove (top)	4.5	2.8			175	574
Tennant Gill Farm	4.5	2.8			80	262
Fountains Fell	3.6	2.2			260	853
Dale Head	3.2	2.0			10	33
Pen-y-ghent	2.1	1.3			275	902
Horton-in-Ribblesdale	5.0	3.1	**22.9**	**14.2**	0	0
Old Ing	6.0	3.7			170	558
Kidhow Gate	7.5	4.7			290	951
Hawes	8.5	5.3	**22.0**	**13.7**	50	164
Hardraw	2.3	1.4			15	49
Great Shunner Fell	7.7	4.8			475	1,558
Thwaite	5.3	3.3			15	49
Keld (Footbridge)	4.6	2.9	**19.9**	**12.4**	170	558
Tan Hill Inn	6.3	3.9			265	869
Trough Heads	8.5	5.3			30	98

Start Point	Distance km	Distance miles	Total km	Total miles	Height gained metres	Height gained feet
Pasture End (A66)	2.0	1.2			50	164
Baldersdale (Bowes Loop)	6.0	3.7	**22.8**	**14.2**	130	427
Grassholme Farm	4.5	2.8			110	361
Middleton B6277	5.3	3.3			155	509
Wynch Bridge	5.5	3.4			50	164
Cronkley Farm	7.0	4.3			145	476
Langdon Beck (Saur Hill Br)	1.7	1.1	**24.0**	**14.9**	15	49
Cow Green (Road bridge)	5.4	3.4			100	328
High Cupgill Head	7.8	4.8			200	656
Dufton (Church)	6.2	3.9	**19.4**	**12.1**	30	98
Knock Old Man	7.0	4.3			640	2,100
Great Dun Fell	2.8	1.7			110	361
Cross Fell	3.4	2.1			180	591
Garrigill (Road)	11.5	7.1			50	164
Alston (Road)	6.8	4.2	**31.5**	**19.4**	30	98
Castle Nook	4.7	2.9			140	459
Slaggyford (A689)	4.2	2.6			30	98
Lambley (A689)	7.1	4.4			180	591
Kellah Burn	3.0	1.9			60	197
Gap Shields Fan (Track)	4.0	2.5			115	377
Greenhead (Railway crossing)	3.1	1.9	**26.1**	**16.2**	20	66
Great Chesters	5.6	3.5			210	689
Peel Road (**Once Brewed**)	5.1	3.2	**10.7**	**6.7**	190	623

Start Point	Distance km	Distance miles	Total km	Total miles	Height gained metres	Height gained feet
Rapishaw Gap	3.5	2.2			130	427
Ladyhill (Road)	8.2	5.1			130	427
Linacres	4.1	2.5			70	230
Ealingham Rigg (Relay Station)	4.2	2.6			170	558
Bellingham (Road)	3.6	2.2	**23.6**	**14.6**	20	66
Hareshaw House (Road)	5.0	3.1			200	656
Whitley Pike	4.9	3.0			135	443
Brownrigg Head	3.8	2.4			120	394
Byrness (A68)	10.7	6.6	**24.4**	**15.1**	100	328
Byrness Hill	1.2	0.7			190	623
Chew Green	6.7	4.2			150	492
Mountain Refuge Hut (804121)	6.2	3.9			140	459
Windy Gyle	6.8	4.2	**20.9**	**13.0**	320	1,050
Clennell Street	1.9	1.2			15	49
Cairn Hill (West Top)	4.7	2.9			240	787
The Schil	5.0	3.1			195	640
Junction (High/ Low route)	1.8	1.1		**0.0**	30	98
Old Halterburnhead	2.1	1.3			0	0
Junction (High/ Low route)	3.1	1.9			10	33
Kirk Yetholm	1.6	1.0	**20.2**	**12.5**	50	164
TOTAL	**409.5**	**254.3**	**409.6**	**254.1**	**11,060**	**36,286**

Loops on the PW

Start Point	Distance km	Distance miles	Height gained metres	Height gained feet
Trough Heads				
Bowes	4.8	3.0	30	98
Baldersdale (main route)	9.1	5.7	150	492
Total	**13.9**	**8.7**	**180**	**590**
Cairn Hill (West Top)				
The Cheviot (return)	3.9	2.4	115	377
Total	**3.9**	**2.4**	**115**	**377**
Junction (High/Low route)				
White Law	2.7	1.7	95	312
Junction (High/Low route)	3.0	1.9	25	82
Total	**5.7**	**3.6**	**120**	**394**

Ordnance Survey Maps List

The following maps can be used to complement the detailed route description provided in this guide.

Ordnance Survey Landranger Map 1:50 000

110	Sheffield & Huddersfield
109	Manchester
103	Blackburn & Burnley
98	Wensleydale & Upper Wharfedale
92	Barnard Castle & Richmond
91	Appleby-in-Westmorland
86	Haltwhistle & Brampton
80	Cheviot Hills & Kielder Water
74	Kelso & Coldstream

Ordnance Survey Explorer Maps 1:25 000

OL1	The Peak District (Dark Peak Area)
OL21	South Pennines (Burnley, Hebden Bridge, Keighley and Todmorden)
OL2	Yorkshire Dales – Southern and Western Areas
OL30	Yorkshire Dales – Northern and Central Areas
OL31	North Pennines – Teesdale and Weardale
OL19	Howgill Fells and Upper Eden Valley
OL43	Hadrian's Wall (Haltwhistle and Hexham)
OL42	Kielder Water and Forest (Bellingham and Simonside Hills)
OL16	The Cheviot Hills (Jedburgh and Wooler)

Geographers A-Z Map Co Ltd

Pennine Way South (A-Z Adventure Atlas)

Pennine Way North (A-Z Adventure Atlas)

(These two publications include 1:25 000 scale Ordnance Survey maps of the complete route in a lightweight and convenient format.)

Pennine Way Publications

It is hard to believe that there are now over fifty publications about the Pennine Way. That is more than one a year for every year since the PW was opened (although to be fair, two were written before 1965!). Sharp eyed readers will note that Tom Stephenson's HMSO guidebook on the PW wasn't published until 1969, which is quite late. The authorities were clearly caught napping there.

It is well worth trying to get a copy of Chris Wright's book published in 1967. You will need the first edition for this, but surprisingly many first editions of PW books can be picked up quite cheaply on the Internet. The exception is Wainwright's book as there were only 2,000 printed for the first edition and there are many Wainwright fans out there who have kept the price well above the original 1968 cover price of eighteen shillings. Although Chris Wright's book is in black and white, it is the OS maps in his book which make it such a treasure. His first edition had all the early PW maps, so you can see where the PW was on the map when (and before) it was opened. Interestingly, the OS got the line of the PW wrong in places and this had to be corrected when the maps were revised.

The fifty-four publications to date on the Pennine Way are detailed below by date, with the most recently published appearing first.

Note: The publication date in brackets is that of the book's first edition (except for book numbers 1, 5 and 11). The Standard Book Numbering (SBN) system was implemented in 1967, and the 10-digit International Standard Book Number (ISBN) was approved as an ISO standard in 1970, however, the 9-digit SBN code was used in the United Kingdom until 1974. Since 1 January 2007, ISBNs have 13 digits. Occasionally, a book may appear without an ISBN, usually if it is printed privately.

1   Bernard Haigh (2013) **The Pennine Way: Our Way** *(2nd edition)* Fastprint pp 226. ISBN 978 1780356464.

2   Peter Stott (2013) **Peter Stott's Pennine Way Memoirs Compiled August 2013** Published privately in A4 format.

3   Geographers A-Z Map Company Ltd (2013) **Pennine Way South (A-Z Adventure Atlas)** pp 64. ISBN 978 1843489610.

4   Geographers A-Z Map Company Ltd (2013) **Pennine Way North (A-Z Adventure Atlas)** pp 68. ISBN 978 1843489603.

5   Alfred Wainwright (Revised by Chris Jesty) (2012) **Pennine Way** *(2nd edition)* Frances Lincoln pp 176. ISBN 978 0 7112 3368 3.

6   Simon Armitage (2012) **Walking Home – Travels with a Troubadour on the Pennine Way** Faber and Faber pp 285. ISBN 978 0 571 24988 6.

7   D.J. Smithers (2012) **36" or Bust! A Pennine Way Challenge** Amazon.co.uk pp 145. ISBN 9781481 077613.

8   Damian Hall (2012) **The Pennine Way** *(Pennine Way National Trail Guide in one single volume)* Aurum Press Ltd pp 189. ISBN 978 1 84513 718 2.

9   Roly Smith (2011) **The Pennine Way** Frances Lincoln Limited pp 112. ISBN 978 0 7112 3024 8.

10 Paddy Dillon (2010) **The Pennine Way** Cicerone pp 219. ISBN 978 1 85284 575 9.

11 Edward de la Billiere, Keith Carter, Chris Scott (2011) **Pennine Way** *(3rd edition Researched and updated by Jim Manthorpe)* Trailblazer Publications pp 269. ISBN 978-1-905864-34-8. (First published 2004 ISBN 1 873756 57 7).

12 Richard Pulk (2007) **Rambles of a Pennine Way-ster** Touchline '99 pp 216. ISBN 978 0 9536646 2 7.

13 Kevin Donkin (2006) **Circular Walks along the Pennine Way** Frances Lincoln Limited pp 367. ISBN 0 71102665 2.

14 Tony Hopkins (2005) **The Pennine Way** Zymurgy Publishing pp160. ISBN 1 903506 13 1.

15 Harvey Maps (2005) **Pennine Way South – Edale to Horton in Ribblesdale** pp 5. ISBN 185137431 0.

16   Harvey Maps (2005) **Pennine Way Central – Horton in Ribblesdale to Greenhead** pp 6. ISBN 185137426 4.

17   Harvey Maps (2005) **Pennine Way North – Greenhead to Kirk Yetholm** pp 5. ISBN 185137421 3.

18   Ueli Hintermeister (1999) **Outdoor Handbuch England: Pennine Way** Conrad Stein pp 155. ISBN 3 89392 164 8.

19   Martin Collins (1998) **The Pennine Way** Cicerone Press pp 136. ISBN 1 85284 262 8.

20   Terry Marsh (1997) **Pennine Way** Dalesman Publishing Company pp190. ISBN 185568 108 0.

21   Mark Wallington (1996) **Pennine Walkies** Hutchinson pp 229. ISBN 0 09 1792347.

22   Peter Gorring, Dilys Cheetham (1995) **Walk this way – The Pennine Way** Gotham Press pp 53. ISBN 0 9526037 0 5.

23   John Gillham (1994) **Pennine Ways. Edale to Kirk Yetholm for the Independent Walker** The Crowood Press Ltd pp 160. ISBN 1 85223 841 0.

24   Harry Penrice (1991) **Daily Outings on The Pennine Way, walks for young and old** Thornhill Press pp 157. ISBN 0 946328 32 3.

25   Frank Duerden (1990) **Great Walks, the Pennine Way** Ward Lock Ltd pp 176. ISBN 0 7063 6813 4.

26   Tony Hopkins (1990) **Pennine Way South – Edale to Bowes** Aurum Press Ltd pp 144. ISBN 1 85410 022 X.

27   Tony Hopkins (1990) **Pennine Way North – Bowes to Kirk Yetholm** Aurum Press Ltd pp 168. ISBN 1 85410 18 1.

28   Chris Harrison (1988) **The Pennine Way Pub Guide** Scarthin Books pp 109. ISBN 0 907758 23 1.

29   Peter Sansom (1988) **On the Pennine Way – Poems from Standedge to Lunedale: 150 miles, or half the Pennine Way** Littlewood Press pp 45. ISBN 0 946407 31 2.

30   Footprint (1988) **The Pennine Way – part one – Edale to Teesdale** pp 8. ISBN 1 871149 01 0.

31   Footprint (1988) **The Pennine Way – part two – Teesdale to Kirk Yetholm** pp 8. ISBN 1 871149 02 9.

32   Pete Bogg (1987) **Laughs along the Pennine Way** Cicerone Press pp 104. ISBN 0902 363 97 2.

33   John J. Fleming (1987) **Day by Day along the Pennine Way – a personal account** Published privately pp 57.

34   Gerard C. De Waal (1987) **Going Dutch – The Pennine Way** GéDéWé pp 174. ISBN 90 800133 1 5 CIP.

35   Barry Pilton (1986) **One Man and his Bog** Corgi Books pp 134. ISBN 0 552 12796 5.

36   Alfred Wainwright (1985) **Wainwright on the Pennine Way** Michael Joseph pp 216. ISBN 0 7181 2429 4.

37   Gerard C. De Waal (1984) **An ode to the Pennine Way** GéDéWé.

38   Graeme Hardy (1983) **North to South along the Pennine Way** Frederick Warne Ltd pp 80. ISBN 0 7232 2813 2.

39   Gerard C. de Waal (1982) **The Pennine Way Ten Voeten Uit** GéDéWé pp 206.

40   Laurie R. Boyle (undated) **The Walk** Published privately pp 45.

41   John Jowett, Rob Mellor, Paul Wilson (undated) **The Pennine Way Pub Guide** Published privately pp 63.

42   Colin Walker (1977) **A Walker on the Pennine Way** Pendyke Publications (Hardback) ISBN 0 904318 10 9.

The above hardback book was originally published in paperback in eight separate sections between March 1974 and May 1975 (see below):

42a   Colin Walker (1975) **A Walker on the Pennine Way – Section Eight – Bellingham to Kirk Yetholm** Pendyke Publications pp 48. ISBN 0 904318 07 9.

42b   Colin Walker (1975) **A Walker on the Pennine Way – Section Seven – Alston to Bellingham** Pendyke Publications pp 48. ISBN 0 904318 06 0.

42c   Colin Walker (1975) **A Walker on the Pennine Way – Section Six – Middleton to Alston** Pendyke Publications pp 48. ISBN 0 904318 05 2.

42d   Colin Walker (1975) **A Walker on the Pennine Way – Section Five – Hawes to Middleton** Pendyke Publications pp 48. ISBN 0 904318 04 4.

42e   Colin Walker (1974) **A Walker on the Pennine Way –
       Section Four – Malham to Hawes** Pendyke Publications
       pp 44. ISBN 0 904318 03 6.

42f   Colin Walker (1974) **A Walker on the Pennine Way
       – Section Three – Ponden to Malham** Pendyke
       Publications pp 44. ISBN 0 904318 02 8.

42g   Colin Walker (1974) **A Walker on the Pennine Way
       – Section Two – Standedge to Ponden** Pendyke
       Publications pp 48. ISBN 0 904318 01 X.

42h   Colin Walker (1974) **A Walker on the Pennine Way
       – Section One – Edale to Standedge** Pendyke
       Publications pp 48. ISBN 0 904308 00 1.

43   Colourmaster (1973) **Read about Walks on the Pennine
       Way** Photo-Precision Limited pp 33. ISBN 0 85933 104 0.

44   John Needham (1971) **The Pennine Way
       Accommodation and Camping Guide** Pennine Way
       Council.

45   Tom Stephenson (1969) **The Pennine Way** HMSO pp 112.
       SBN 11 7004804.

46   J.H.B. Peel (1969) **Along the Pennine Way** Cassell &
       Company Ltd pp 204. ISBN 304 93331 7.

47   Michael Marriott (1968) **The Shell Book of the Pennine
       Way** The Queen Anne Press Ltd pp 80.

48   Alfred Wainwright (1968) **Pennine Way Companion** pub
       Westmorland Gazette pp 224. (Michael Joseph edition
       1992 ISBN 0718140710.)

49   James Haworth [ed.] (1967) **The Pennine Way and Walks
       in Derbyshire** Derbyshire Countryside Ltd pp 64.

50   Christopher J. Wright (1967) **A guide to the Pennine
       Way** Constable & Co Ltd pp 252. (1981 edition ISBN 0 09
       462760 6.)

51   H.O. Wade (1966) **The Pennine Way in Twenty Days**
       Harold Hill pp 72.

52   Alan P. Binns (1966) **Walking the Pennine Way** H.
       Gerrard Ltd pp 87. (Frederick Warne edition ISBN 7232
       2803 5.)

53   Kenneth Oldham (1960) **The Pennine Way** The Dalesman Publishing Company pp 70. (1982 edition ISBN 0 85206 691 0.)

54   John D. Wood (1947) **Mountain Trail – The Pennine Way from the Peak to the Cheviot** George Allen & Unwin pp 240.

At the time of going to press, there were three Kindle eBooks on the Pennine Way. These are not guide books but the authors' accounts or personal diaries.

Dean Carter **End to End – An Adventure on the Pennine Way** [Kindle Edition]

File Size: 2845 Kb [26 Aug 2013] ASIN: B00ET98L5O

D. J. Smithers **36″ or Bust! A Pennine Way challenge** [Kindle Edition]

File Size: 211 Kb [30 April 2012] ASIN: B007ZAZ8Y6

Anorak on the Pennine Way [Kindle Edition]

File Size: 273 Kb ASIN: B00ECHGTUW

The Pennine Way Association

The original Pennine Way Association, set up as a result of the 1938 Conference, was dissolved when the Pennine Way was opened in 1965.

In 1970, representatives of the Ramblers' Association emphasised the need for a single organisation to act as a *"focus of public interest in Britain's first and most famous long-distance footpath."* The Pennine Way Council (PWC) first met in 1971, and Tom Stephenson, then President of the Ramblers' Association, was elected as first Chairman of the Council, an office he vacated in 1974 to become President. It provided a forum for the coming together of voluntary bodies, highway authorities and individual users.

Twenty years after the Pennine Way Council was formed, events had moved on with the Countryside Commission's (now Natural England) deeper involvement in the overall plan for the maintenance of the Pennine Way. There was a view that this change meant that the Council had served its purpose and should cease to function. An alternative perspective was that there should be a change to an association status, with such a body continuing to do what it had done well, namely to provide a forum for interested parties; an advisory route enquiry service; an accommodation guide and biannual newsletters.

The name the Pennine Way Association (PWA) was therefore agreed and adopted at the Annual General Meeting of the PWC held on the 11 April 1992. The current PWA aims are:

> *'To secure the protection of the Pennine Way, to provide information about the Way to the public, to educate users of the Way and its environs in a proper respect for the countryside, to assist the organisation of voluntary effort directed at the maintenance of the*

Way, and to provide a forum in which different interests connected with the Way and its use can discuss problems of mutual concern.'

©Pennine Way Association

Further information about activities of the Pennine Way Association can be found at: *http://www.penninewayassociation.co.uk*

About the author

Chris at Deer Play on the Pennine Way
(Land's End to John o' Groats Walk 2003)

Chris Sainty's passion with the Pennine Way started during his college education where he developed an interest in walking. On 11 September 1975, he set off from Kirk Yetholm with the intention of seeing how far he could walk along this National Trail. Blisters at Alston forced Chris to retire from the PW, on that occasion, but the seed was sown and he was back in April 1977 when he completed the full route from Edale to Kirk Yetholm.

Over the subsequent years, Chris has walked the PW a further nine times, either as a single journey, or over a number of shorter trips to cover the full distance. In the early days when his walking experience was still in its infancy, key attractions of the PW were the people he walked with on the route, as well as the fact that it could be split into weekly sections, with accommodation and transport easily available.

You may wonder what has drawn Chris back to the Pennine Way so often. The combination of diverse landscapes along the route; seasonal and climatic variations; together with the personal physical and mental experience, makes every visit unique.

Chris joined the Pennine Way Council (now the Pennine Way Association) as an associate member in 1980 following a meeting with the then Secretary Ron McLoughlin (R.A. Manchester representative), at Baldersdale youth hostel, whilst on his sixth visit back to the Pennine Way. He was encouraged to become Honorary Secretary in 1981, at the age of twenty-six, and he held this post until 2002. In March 2000 he took on the additional role of Editor of the Pennine Way Association's biannual newsletter which he relinquished in 2008. Chris was elected Chairman for a year in 2008, returning to this role again in 2013.

The Pennine Way: A Walker's Guide, started off as a personal project. It has developed, however, into a guide which Chris hopes will be of interest not only to walkers, but to those curious about the history of the Pennine Way.

ND - #0031 - 270225 - C6 - 197/128/13 - PB - 9781780913797 - Gloss Lamination